Selected Poems

Pablo Neruda

Edited by Nathaniel Tarn
Translated by Anthony Kerrigan,
W. S. Merwin, Alastair Reid
and Nathaniel Tarn
with an Introduction by
Jean Franco

Penguin Books

Penguin Books Ltd, Harmondsworth,
Middlesex, England
Penguin Books, 625 Madison Avenue,
New York, New York 10022, U.S.A.
Penguin Books Australia Ltd, Ringwood,
Victoria, Australia
Penguin Books Canada Ltd, 2801 John Street,
Markham, Ontario, Canada L3R 1B4
Penguin Books (N.Z.) Ltd, 182–190 Wairau Road, Auckland 10, New Zealand

These translations first published by Jonathan Cape 1970
Published in Penguin Books 1975
Reprinted 1977, 1979

Translations copyright © Anthony Kerrigan,
W. S. Merwin, Alastair Reid and Nathaniel Tarn, 1970, 1975
Introduction copyright © Jean Franco, 1975
All rights reserved

Made and printed in Great Britain by
Hazell Watson & Viney Ltd,
Aylesbury, Bucks
Set in Monotype Bembo

The Penguin Poets
Pablo Neruda

Pablo Neruda, the internationally acclaimed Latin American poet, was born in 1904 in Parral, Chile. In 1920 he went to Santiago to study and published his first book of poems, *La canción de la fiesta* (1921); and his second collection, *Crepusculario* (1923), brought him instant recognition. In 1924 he published the enormously popular *Veinte poemas de amor y una canción desesperada*. From 1927 to 1945 he served as Chilean consul in Rangoon, Java and Barcelona, and was writing continuously. Greatly influenced by events in the Spanish Civil War, Neruda joined the Communist Party after the Second World War, and his changed attitudes registered themselves in his poetry. From now on he regarded his poetry not as an elite pursuit but as a statement of human solidarity addressed to 'simple people'. *Canto general* (one part of which is *The Heights of Macchu Picchu*, translated by Nathaniel Tarn) is a poem of epic proportions, tracing the history of Latin America and evoking the grandeur of its landscapes. It also introduces political polemic. Always a prolific poet, Neruda continued to write poetry throughout the fifties and sixties, and in 1971 he was awarded the Nobel Prize for Poetry. From 1970 to 1973 he served under Allende as Chilean ambassador to Paris.

Pablo Neruda died in 1973, shortly after the coup in Chile which ousted Allende.

Contents

Contents

Editor's Foreword

The present selection represents a reduced model of the *Selected Poems* of Pablo Neruda, published by Jonathan Cape, London, in 1970 and Delacorte Press/ Seymour Lawrence, Boston-New York in 1971. This, in turn, had been based on a list provided by Pablo Neruda in July 1965 at the P.E.N. Conference in Bled, Yugoslavia. It may be worth noting that, at the time, Mr Neruda did not include any of his more outspoken political poems, no doubt biding his time for a more adequate treatment of these on another occasion. I have tried here to keep roughly the same balance in the coverage of individual volumes and in contributions by the four translators as prevailed in the earlier work. It will be noticed that the translators shared out the work along lines of previous interests, made manifest, in part, in the bibliography below. The basic Spanish text used in most cases was the second edition of the *Obras Completas*, Losada, Buenos Aires, 1962.

The acknowledgements go, as before, to the late Pablo Neruda himself for giving this venture his blessing, to Mr Alastair Reid for considerable editorial help in London and to Mr Rafael Nadal for looking over the larger manuscript in its near final stage.

Plans are now afoot, especially in the United States, to translate Pablo Neruda book by book: the 'Selected' stage is over and we move on towards the 'Collected' poems in English. In the meantime, the following list of books, mostly available in paperback (it is not exhaustive), may be of use to readers of this volume. They are nearly all bilingual.

Princeton, May 1972   NATHANIEL TARN

Twenty Love Poems & a Song of Despair, trans. W. S. Merwin, Cape Editions, London, and Grossman, New York, 1969.

The Man Who Told His Love (an 'imitation' of *Twenty Love Poems & a Song of Despair*), trans. Christopher Logue, in C. Logue, *Songs*, Scorpion Press, 1959.

The Heights of Macchu Picchu, trans. Nathaniel Tarn with an introduction by R. Pring Mill, Farrar Straus, New York, 1967 and Jonathan Cape Paperbacks, London, 1972.

We Are Many, trans. Alastair Reid, Cape Goliard, London, and Grossman, New York, 1969.

Extravagaria, trans. Alastair Reid, Jonathan Cape Poetry Paperbacks, London, 1972.

Selected Poems of Pablo Neruda, trans. and ed. by Ben Belitt with an introduction by Luis Monguió, Grove Press, New York, 1961.

Pablo Neruda: A New Decade: Poems 1958–1967, ed. and introduced by Ben Belitt, trans. Ben Belitt and Alastair Reid, Grove Press, New York, 1969.

Neruda and Vallejo: Selected Poems, ed. Robert Bly, trans. Robert Bly and James Wright, Beacon Press, Boston, 1971.

The Penguin Book of Socialist Verse, ed. Alan Bold (uses some Bly–Wright material), Penguin Books, Harmondsworth, 1970.

The Penguin Book of Modern Verse Translation (reprinted as *Poem into Poem*, 1970), ed. George Steiner (uses some Logue and Tarn material), Penguin Books, Harmondsworth, 1966.

Pablo Neruda is like Emerson's poet in that he 'puts eyes and tongues into every dumb and inanimate object' and 'as the eyes of Lyncaeus were said to see the earth so the poet turns the world to glass and shows us all things in their right series and process'. So too Neruda wants a poetry that breaks 'the wall of silence round crystal, wood and stone', that strives after a 'knowledge without antecedents'. Yet he is not merely or primarily a poet of nature. 'Qui dit poète, dit en même temps et nécessairement historien et philosophe,' wrote Hugo, and Neruda's poetry, like that of the great Orphic poets – Dante, Milton, Whitman and the Hugo of *La Légende des siècles* – is bound by a coherent vision of man and the universe, a *mythos* which allowed him to conceive and write the total poem, the *Canto general*, the *General Song*. Just as we cannot separate Dante and Milton from their theology nor Hugo and Whitman from the idea of democracy and progress so we cannot take Neruda's poetry without the political nettle, without the vision of unalienated man, of justice and equality on earth. For it is this which has enabled him to become a public poet, to address himself to a community not simply as an individual but as their voice; it has given substance to his prophecy and provided the key to his deciphering of the universe. The visions of Dante and Milton were backed by Christianity, Whitman and Hugo derived their energy from the people; and in the twentieth century, it has been poets like Aimé Césaire and Neruda who have been able to stand up against the current mistrust of 'great speech' and assume a vatic role, Césaire because of his *négritude* and Neruda because of the untapped energies of a hitherto disinherited America.

It must be allowed nevertheless that Neruda's sensibility to nature is unique in Spanish American poetry, that the poet laureate of the masses is also the poet of empty space – of America before man, or the solitary Antarctic:

> your breast of peace polished by the wind
> like a pure rectangle of quartz,
> and the un-breathed, the infinite
> transparent material, the opened air,
> the solitude without earth or poverty.
>   ('Antarctic')

This sensibility was formed by a frontier childhood less common in Southern America than in the North. Neruda was, in fact, born Neftalí Reyes in 1904 in Parral and in 1906 was taken to the then frontier town of Temuco in southern Chile, an area that was still a pioneer region, having been opened up at the turn of the century as a result of a pact with the Araucanian Indians. His father was involved in that encroachment on the forest by progress and civilization and his job – the laying of new railway tracks – assumes symbolic proportions in Neruda's personal mythology in which, ever afterwards, the linear drive, the male thrust represents the essential dynamics in man's transcendence of the cyclical process of nature. The father and step-mother saw the 'first locomotive, the first cattle and the first vegetables of that virgin region of cold and tempest'. Here, too, around the year 1914, during the long, rainy winter, Neruda composed his first poems:

> and something started in my soul,
> fever or forgotten wings,
> and I made my own way,
> deciphering
> that fire,
> and I wrote the first faint line,
> faint, without substance, pure
> nonsense,
> pure wisdom
> of someone who knows nothing,
> and suddenly I saw
> the heavens
> unfastened
> and open.

('Poetry')

Neruda's vocation as a poet was born here, in this region where he grew up unhampered by social and religious conventions or established literary schools (one of his friends was the first man ever to write poetry south of the river Bío Bío), nourished by a landscape in which he seemed the only discoverer, the namer of plants and insects, living, as he later described it, in a perpetual state of wonder.

At the age of sixteen, when he left Temuco, to become a lonely student in Santiago, he was already a poet and had already stamped the signature 'Pablo Neruda' on his work. More than any other single gesture, this assumption of a pseudonym with its echoes of the Evangelist and the surname of the then well-known Czech writer, Jan Neruda, signified a refusal to be limited by his provincial background. He was to become the poet of Chile or the poet of America but not merely the poet of Temuco. His second collection of poems, *Veinte poemas de amor* (*Twenty Poems of Love*, 1924), though it did not go into a second edition until 1932, gave him a national reputation when he was barely twenty. Now translated into many languages, the poems are familiar to Latin Americans in the way that proverbs or popular songs are, though familiarity cannot deprive them of their freshness and energy. For these are poems of discovery. They tell of the adolescent's confrontation of woman and the universe and his sense of estrangement. In them, the woman (there were in fact two women addressed in the poems, one from Santiago, the other from Temuco) merges into nature, is metamorphosed into earth or mist with the poet facing her as interrogator and explorer, defining himself against an entire universe. Yet his urge to codify, to name and discover, cannot overcome the sense of mystery:

> Who writes your name in letters of smoke among the stars of the south?
> Oh let me remember you as you were before you existed.
>
> ('Every Day You Play')

This interrogation of the other, this writing of the name he has deciphered from the enigma, will become a recurrent attitude in his poetry as will his identification of woman with cosmic nature.

From the publication of the *Twenty Poems of Love* in 1924 to his appointment as consul in Barcelona in 1934, Neruda's story is bizarre and his writing the fruit of isolation. Always prolific, he published a novel, *El habitante y su esperanza* (*The Inhabitant and His Hope*), and a collection of poems, *Tentativa del hombre infinito* (*The Trying of Infinite Man*), in 1926. In 1927, he was appointed to a diplomatic post in Rangoon and for five years lived in the East, serving in Rangoon, Colombo and Java and all the time cut off from spoken Spanish and lonely to the point of desperation, reduced, he declares in a letter to a friend, to picking up stray dogs for company. In addition to isolation, he suffered the tragi-comic indignities of impoverished respectability, for his salary depended on the amount of consular business he dispatched. India he will later remember with distaste:

> naked and elegant buddhas
> smiling at the cocktail party
> of empty eternity.
>
> ('Religion in the East')

In a poem written in 1967, 'The Watersong Ends', Neruda recalls visiting Vietnam at this time and being stranded in the jungle, 'twenty years old, waiting for death, shrinking into my language'. And though he also recalls the sense of fraternity he felt on that occasion, it is the isolation which at the time was translated into his poetry. During his stay in the East and even before his departure from Chile, men and objects had become opaque, unresponsive. 'I feel that things have found their own expression,' he wrote in a letter to his friend, Eandi, 'and that I have no part in them nor have I power to penetrate them.' The poems of this period were published in Spain as *Residencia en la tierra* (*Residence on Earth*), the first volume of which (there were to be three) appeared in 1933. They are poems which produce a dis-ordering of the world, as objects, sense-impressions, nature are fleetingly glimpsed in their procession towards death. A later Neruda would consider them aberrant though they have recently found an eloquent defender in the Argentine novelist, Julio Cortázar. In fact they are probably nearer the mood of our age than anything he wrote since, for in them there is the suggestion (now a commonplace perception) that man, a recent invention, is destined to disappear and that whatever laws exist in the universe, they are not human ones. *Residence* presents us with a world that resists teleology, one in which there is no ultimate design. Objects, once pliable to the poet's organization, now become strange, lose their solidity whilst the poet lends his ear:

> to the pure circulation, to the increase,
> without direction giving way to what is approaching,
> to what issues forth dressed in chains and carnations.
> ('Weak with the Dawn')

That problematic entity, the 'I', as diffuse and ephemeral as rain, can no longer claim Orphic powers, can no longer address an oracular world which will yield its meaning to his interrogation. Rather there is a 'lurch of objects calling without answers, with a truceless movement, a name I can't make out' ('Ars Poetica'). That Neruda afterwards looks back on this part of his life as a fall is obvious from numerous references in his poetry; certainly, it is the one time in his life when he finds no answers in the objective world. Yet even as he fails to envisage anything grander than a futile individual existence, he repudiates this trivial destiny:

> I do not want to be the inheritor of so many misfortunes.
> I do not want to continue as a root and as a tomb,
> as a solitary tunnel, as a cellar full of corpses,
> stiff with cold, dying with pain.
> ('Walking Around')

What happens next is what enabled the *Canto general*, Neruda's major poem, to be written. It is nothing less than a kind of resurrection during which order and meaning again flow into the universe. The process begins in Spain where Neruda, as Chilean consul first in Barcelona, then in Madrid, found himself living in a community of poets who had a sense of their relationship with the people. Neruda's initial involvement in politics had much to do with his friendship with Rafael Alberti, whose home was destroyed by Fascists in 1934, and with Lorca, whose assassination soon after the outbreak of the Civil War in 1936 drew a passionate protest from Neruda together with the statement that he did not consider himself to be a political poet. Yet he lost his post as consul because of his involvement in the struggle and the sense of personal outrage at destruction flows into a political confrontation:

> Treacherous
> generals:
> see my dead house,
> look at broken Spain:

from every house burning metal flows
instead of flowers.
                (ꞌIꞌm Explaining a Few Thingsꞌ)

In these poems of *España en el corazón* (*Spain in my Heart*, 1938) Neruda dis-
covers the power of ꞌgreat speechꞌ and though he had not yet begun to read his
poems aloud, they are unmistakably addressed to an audience. These poems
were never intended to be merely script or signs on a printed page but were to
be uttered and declaimed in order to elicit a response. This distinction between
written and spoken poetry is important, for the conception that poetry is a form
of utterance and therefore a public rather than a private act influenced Nerudaꞌs
development. Very much later, in *Plenos poderes* (*Full Powers*, 1962), he was to
write, ꞌFor human beings, not to speak is to dieꞌ and ꞌI utter and I amꞌ (The
Word). In *Residence*, he had lost any sense of anotherꞌs presence, his dialogue
being with a dying universe. The change therefore was dramatic when in ꞌIꞌm
Explaining a Few Thingsꞌ he began the poem as if questioned by a plural ꞌyouꞌ,
as if the world had suddenly been repopulated with people he must both address
and accuse.

   This sense of a public, this defining of the people to whom his poetry com-
municates, becomes more specific after 1938, the year in which he began to
conceive of the Chilean epic that would turn into the *Canto general*. This
fifteen-section poem was published in 1950 and during the twelve years of
its composition Neruda had become a militant. For three of those years, from
1940 to 1943, he lived outside Chile in Mexico, where he served as consul, but
from 1945, when he was elected Senator and joined the Communist Party, he was
constantly involved with workers and ordinary people. In 1948 the President of
Chile, González Videla, whose candidature had been supported by the Com-
munist Party, broke off relations with several Eastern European countries.
Neruda, openly critical, found himself threatened with arrest and went into
hiding, moving from house to house, sheltered by workers and country people.
Section X of the *Canto general*, ꞌEl fugitivoꞌ (The Fugitive), is devoted to this
experience in which he shared the homes of the workers for whom his poetry
was intended. Already before this, on his return from Spain, he had begun to
read his poetry aloud at trade union meetings and political rallies and he later
described the first of such readings as ꞌthe most important fact in my literary
careerꞌ. Certainly they contributed to the final form of the *Canto general* in
which the language belongs to the heightened form of speech used in oratory,
ceremony or invective. The poem breaks away from the concept of an élite
or minority poetry without resorting to the language of daily life, using in-
stead the arts of rhetoric. But it is also an Orphic poem which unfolds the secret
pattern of nature and history, which reveals the true story of the Americas, ex-
plains their geography, the oppression of their peoples by conquerors and
dictators, and terminates with the poetꞌs autobiography. Its range includes

descriptive poetry, polemic, satire, eulogy, insult, panegyric and lament. Throughout, Neruda is the mediator, he who hears the voice of nature and the past, who deciphers the enigma of stone or listens to the secret tongue of rivers and forests:

> Now talk to me, Bío Bío,
> ... you gave
> me the language, the night-time song
> mingled with rain and foliage.

Nature and history become the oracles which offer the key to human destiny, showing how the material of progress can also be the instrument of exploitation teaching that man's fate is in his own hands, in his ability to make a good life through work. This addressing of nature and history to penetrate their occult significance recurs in each section of the poem but nowhere more powerfully than in *The Heights of Macchu Picchu*, where, meditating on the Inca fortress which for centuries lay hidden in the Andean mountains and on its vast, mysterious structures, Neruda brings the past to life and makes the stones speak of those who built and laboured. As in the Spain poems, he presents himself as the witness, as the man who has seen and touched and now transmits the truth to others:

> I see the ancient being, the slave, the sleeping one,
> blanket his fields – a body, a thousand bodies, a man, a thousand
> women swept by the sable whirlwind, charred with rain and night.
> (Section XI of *The Heights of Macchu Picchu*)

The poet is always there – touching, showing, seeing – 'I *question* you, salt of the highways', '*Look* at them now, *touch* this substance', 'I *saw* you, night of the sea', 'Suddenly I *saw* the environs intensely populated'. The examples could be multiplied. Neruda is truly the evangelist here, persuading through his own example.

But *Canto general* also re-enacts that significant moment when Neruda confronted a natural world that still awaited the human imprint. This moment of genesis when consciousness emerged from darkness, when buildings, words and artefacts came into existence, represents one of the privileged instances of individual and social history. In a much later poem, *La espada encendida* (*The Flaming Sword*, 1970), Neruda was to relate the genesis as myth, telling of the expulsion of the primal pair from Eden, the death of God and their realization that man and woman are the true gods of their own destiny. In *Canto general*, it is not by way of myth, but by describing the patterns of nature and history that Neruda traces this decisive act. He goes back time and time again to that step whether in his own life or in the remote past when men first separated their destiny from the cycle of nature. And he finds particularly significant those monuments of primitive man on which the human hand just manages to lay its imprint as evidence of man's passage on the earth. So he describes the stones of Rapa Nui on which:

> ... the faces of man appeared
> issuing from the matrix of islands,
> born from the empty craters
> their feet entwined in silence.
>
> They were the sentinels and they closed
> the cycle of the waters that surged
> from all the wet domains.
>
> ('Rapa Nui')

Like the Magnificat, the *Canto general* exalts those of low degree – the just and the constructors – and conversely consigns to oblivion those who have betrayed. Here invective and insult – by no means as alien to poetry as might be imagined – have their place. The curse falls on González Videla, on the exploiters of Chile, on the tyrants and dictators, on 'celestial poets', and these ritual insults, like those uttered by ancient warriors, are destined to achieve a reversal of fortune. The dead will be born again; those who have triumphed will slip into silence and be destroyed.

It is futile, nevertheless, to reduce the *Canto general* to a recital of themes or a cataloguing of imagery, for whilst the poem gives a sense of organization, of a powerful and coherent view of nature and history, it is also a poem whose very energy and variety, whose very detail, is as important as the whole. Its effect is not that of abstraction but rather of proliferation; the energy is conveyed through the very accumulation of imagery so that even a description of a drowned man takes on vitality:

> ... dishevelled and divided,
> like an oozing stem, he is the escutcheon
> of the tide, a suit triturated
> by the amethysts, a wounded inheritance
> under the sea, on the numerous tree.
>
> ('The Fish and the Drowned Man')

After the publication of the *Canto general*, Neruda became increasingly pre-occupied with clarity, with the communication of his poetry to a non-literary public, and this led him to the composition of his *Odas elementales* (*Elemental Odes*, 1954, complete edition 1957). The short lines of these poems mark a development away from the ceremonial and from oratory and towards a poetry intended to be as natural as song; indeed, he wishes to suggest an art as close as possible to life. Yet he is disingenuous when he writes:

> Book, let me go.
> I won't go clothed
> in volumes,
> I don't come out
> of collected works,
> my poems
> have not eaten poems –
> they devour
> exciting happenings.

The odes are a homage to daily living, to ordinary people and objects. They celebrate bread, wood, tomatoes, the weather, clothes and the elements. There is none of that horror of the banal or the quotidian which one finds in certain Surrealists, perhaps because Neruda's ordinary people belong to some stage before the conveyor belt and the assembly line. They are sailors, bricklayers, miners, carpenters or bakers – all those who work involves the handling of primary materials. The odes restore a sense of the wholesomeness of work and at the same time suggest that Neruda's utopia is perhaps not very different from the community in which he grew up.

As in the *Canto general*, the language of the odes implies an attitude to the word which is different from that held by many contemporary writers whose distrust of language reduces them to silence. Not so Neruda who not only regards the word as a communion vessel with the past but also as the giver of life:

> ... the word fills with meaning.
> It remained gravid and it filled up with lives.
> Everything had to do with births and sounds –
> affirmation, clarity, strength,
> negation, destruction, death –
> the verb took over all the power
> and blended existence with essence
> in the electricity of its beauty.

('The Word')

So the word gives 'glass-quality to glass, blood to blood' and the act of naming becomes inseparable from consciousness of the world.

Though Neruda views poetry as a social act, this by no means limits his range. He has always sought to record his own experience as directly as possible and a vast amount of his poetry is autobiographical. He has also resorted to the mythical or the fabulous, as in some of the poems in the collection *Estravagario* (1958) such as the 'Fable of the Mermaid and the Drunks' or the 'Furious Struggle between Seamen and an Octopus of Colossal Size'. And there has been an astonishing revival of love poetry, first in his *Versos del capitán* (*The Captain's Verses*, 1952), a collection published anonymously in Naples and only publicly acknowledged as his own in 1962. This purports to be addressed to Rosario de la Cerda but in reality the poems were written as a tribute to Matilde Urrutia whom he married in 1955 and to whom he addressed the *Cien sonetos de amor* (*One Hundred Sonnets of Love*) in 1959.

At this point, Neruda's poetry (perhaps with his marriage) underwent a further metamorphosis as he began to write more and more intensely of nature, of the ocean, of his house at Isla Negra. After so many wanderings, the traveller appeared to come to rest, to enter into an almost religious communion with the natural world. He published poems on the birds of Chile (*Arte de pájaros*, 1966), on the stones of Chile (*Las piedras de Chile*, 1961), on his house (*Una casa en la arena*, 1966), and he drew up an inventory of his life in the long autobiographical collection, *Memorial de Isla Negra* (1964). In this poetry of the sixties, Neruda is once again the Orphic poet, now once more explores the mystery of nature. It is as if on a shrinking planet, Neruda wishes to restore a sense of wonder, of the sacredness of the natural world. So he sees the stones of Chile not only as material to be used in human constructions but as 'mysterious, unearthly matter', planetary in their origin, and eloquent of a universe unknown to man. In *Estravagario*, he had declared that he did not want to name things but 'to mix them up':

> until all light in the world
> has the oneness of the ocean,
> a generous, vast wholeness,
> a crackling, living fragrance.
> ('Too Many Names')

Though he did not stop writing political and historical poetry, in this too there is a sense of his returning to essences, to his origins. In *Cantos ceremoniales* (*Ceremonial Songs*, 1961), he writes:

> ... I stripped in the light,
> I let my hands fall to the sea,
> and when everything took on transparency,
> under the land, I was at peace.
> ('Fiesta's End')

Neruda once drew an analogy between the profession of the poet and that of the boatman who guides his boat along the current of time. In these later years, he speaks increasingly of his glimpse of the ocean of death and fittingly he named a recent collection *La barcarola* (*The Watersong*, 1967). These are poems in which he takes stock of his life, speaking of his wanderings, his political involvement and his personal happiness. Remarkably, this poet who had expressed the aggressive confidence of adolescence in the *Twenty Poems of Love* and the mature vision of the *Canto general* now views death with grace if not with joy:

It is time, love, to break off that sombre rose,
shut up the stars and bury the ash in the earth;
and, in the rising of the light, wake with those who awoke
or go on in the dream, reaching the other shore of the sea which has no other shore.

('The Watersong Ends')

This selection of Neruda's poetry in translation can only hope to offer some samples of the many phases and facets of his poetry. Appropriately, 'The Watersong Ends' of 1967, with its valedictory note, is the final poem in this brief anthology. Yet Neruda's life and poetry continued and took new directions. In 1967, he had already published a musical play (a completely new genre for him), *Fulgor y muerte de Joaquín Murieta* (*Death and Apotheosis of Joaquín Murieta*), which dealt with a Californian folk hero supposedly of Chilean origin; and in 1970, he wrote a myth poem on the genesis of human progress, *La espada encendida*. With the election of Allende to the Presidency of the country in 1970, Chile took a decisive step towards realizing the socially just society in which the poet believed. Indeed, he was himself official Communist Party candidate for the Presidency before a coalition agreed to nominate Allende. After the election, he once again left Isla Negra, this time for Paris where he was appointed Ambassador and where he was living in 1971 when he was awarded the Nobel prize. Unlike Sartre, he accepted the award, an acceptance which was consistent with his view of the poet's role as a spokesman of the people.

Prolific as ever, he published 'Four French poems' in 1972 and, in the same year, *Geografía infructuosa* (*Fruitless Geography*). However, soon after receiving the prize, he returned to Isla Negra, already a sick man, believing that he had earned his retirement to 'winter quarters'. He found himself, instead, in a country already on the edge of civil war. 'This is a heart-rending moment for Chile,' he declared in an interview with his long-time friend and biographer, Margarita Aguirre, 'it invades my study and there is no option but to go on participating in this great struggle.' Long experience of Chilean politics made him singularly aware of the imminence of the tragic confrontation. In the same interview, published in August 1973, he described what was happening as a 'silent Vietnam without bombs or gunfire . . . But otherwise, every possible weapon is being used inside and outside the country against Chile. We are at this very moment fighting an undeclared war.' On 11 September, as he lay mortally sick in Isla Negra, the navy rebelled, then the army. La Moneda palace was bombed and Allende killed. Neruda had lived long enough to see the results of half a century of struggle liquidated. He died on 23 September. Fittingly, his funeral became the first public demonstration against the military government; and not surprisingly, his house in Santiago was broken into and many of the books and papers there destroyed.

His last poems are full of prescient irony. Early in 1973, he had published the *Incitación al Nixonicidio y alabanza de la revolución chilena* (*Incitement to Nixonicide and Celebration of the Chilean Revolution*) in which he had recourse to 'the most ancient weapons of poetry – the song and the broadsheet which had been used by both classical and romantic poets against the enemy'. Despite the fury of the title, it is one of the most consciously literary of his collections, rich in references to other poets and other texts, to Whitman, Quevedo and to the sixteenth-century poet Alonso de Ercilla y Zúñiga who wrote the first Chilean epic, *La Araucana*. It is as if he were shoring up his defences against the approach of barbarism. Just before he died, the Buenos Aires magazine, *Crisis*, published a group of poems which grin astonishingly in the face of death, a latter-day *Estravagario*, recording his struggles with the dictionary, and including odd fantasies like the expulsion of the Ostrogoth family from their house and garden by an army of corpses, or the vision of a world flooded by a 'great urinator'. On the edge of the final silence, Neruda writes his own best epitaph, the epitaph of an 'animal of light' who has exhausted all that can be said in words:

> And today in the depth of the lost forest
> he hears the sound of the enemy and runs away
> not from the others but from himself
> from that interminable conversation
> from the chorus which always accompanied us
> and from the meaning of life.
>
> Because this once, because just once, because
> a syllable or an interval of silence
> or the unstifled noise of a wave
> leave me face to face with the truth
> and there is nothing more to interpret,
> nothing more to say; this was everything.
> Closed were the forest doors.
> The sun goes round opening up the leaves
> The moon appears like a white fruit
> and man bows to his destiny.

Stanford University, 1973   JEAN FRANCO

from *Veinte poemas de amor* (1924)

Juegas todos los días con la luz del universo.
Sutil visitadora, llegas en la flor y en el agua.
Eres más que esta blanca cabecita que aprieto
como un racimo entre mis manos cada día.

A nadie te pareces desde que yo te amo.
Déjame tenderte entre guirnaldas amarillas.
Quién escribe tu nombre con letras de humo entre las estrellas del sur?
Ah déjame recordarte cómo eras entonces, cuando aún no existías.

De pronto el viento aúlla y golpea mi ventana cerrada.
El cielo es una red cuajada de peces sombríos.
Aquí vienen a dar todos los vientos, todos.
Se desviste la lluvia.

Pasan huyendo los pájaros.
El viento. El viento.
Yo sólo puedo luchar contra la fuerza de los hombres.
El temporal arremolina hojas oscuras
y suelta todas las barcas que anoche amarraron al cielo.

Tú estás aquí. Ah tú no huyes.
Tú me responderás hasta el último grito.
Ovíllate a mi lado como si tuvieras miedo.
Sin embargo alguna vez corrió una sombra extraña por tus ojos.

Ahora, ahora también, pequeña, me traes madreselvas,
y tienes hasta los senos perfumados.
Mientras el viento triste galopa matando mariposas
yo te amo, y mi alegría muerde tu boca de ciruela.

Cuánto te habrá dolido acostumbrarte a mí,
a mi alma sola y salvaje, a mi nombre que todos ahuyentan.
Hemos visto arder tantas veces el lucero besándonos los ojos
y sobre nuestras cabezas destorcerse los crepúsculos en abanicos girantes.

Mis palabras llovieron sobre ti acariciándote.
Amé desde hace tiempo tu cuerpo de nácar soleado.
Hasta te creo dueña del universo.

XIV *Every Day You Play...*

Every day you play with the light of the universe.
Subtle visitor, you arrive in the flower and the water.
You are more than this white head that I hold tightly
as a bunch of flowers, every day, between my hands.

You are like nobody since I love you.
Let me spread you out among yellow garlands.
Who writes your name in letters of smoke among the stars of the south?
Oh let me remember you as you were before you existed.

Suddenly the wind howls and bangs at my shut window.
The sky is a net crammed with shadowy fish.
Here all the winds let go sooner or later, all of them.
The rain takes off her clothes.

The birds go by, fleeing.
The wind. The wind.
I alone can contend against the power of men.
The storm whirls dark leaves
and turns loose all the boats that were moored last night to the sky.

You are here. Oh, you do not run away.
You will answer me to the last cry.
Curl round me as though you were frightened.
Even so, a strange shadow once ran through your eyes.

Now, now too, little one, you bring me honeysuckle,
and even your breasts smell of it.
While the sad wind goes slaughtering butterflies
I love you, and my happiness bites the plum of your mouth.

How you must have suffered getting accustomed to me,
my savage, solitary soul, my name that sends them all running.
So many times we have seen the morning star burn, kissing our eyes,
and over our heads the grey light unwind in turning fans.

My words rained over you, stroking you.
A long time I have loved the sunned mother-of-pearl of your body.
Until I even believe that you own the universe.

Te traeré de las montañas flores alegres, copihues,
avellanas oscuras, y cestas silvestres de besos.
Quiero hacer contigo
lo que la primavera hace con los cerezos.

I will bring you happy flowers from the mountains, bluebells,
dark hazels, and rustic baskets of kisses.
I want
to do with you what spring does with the cherry trees.

[W.S.M.]

Puedo escribir los versos más tristes esta noche.

Escribir, por ejemplo: 'La noche está estrellada,
y tiritan, azules, los astros, a lo lejos'.

El viento de la noche gira en el cielo y canta.

Puedo escribir los versos más tristes esta noche.
Yo la quise, y a veces ella también me quiso.

En las noches como ésta la tuve entre mis brazos.
La besé tantas veces bajo el cielo infinito.

Ella me quiso, a veces yo también la quería.
Cómo no haber amado sus grandes ojos fijos.

Puedo escribir los versos más tristes esta noche.
Pensar que no la tengo. Sentir que la he perdido.

Oír la noche inmensa, más inmensa sin ella.
Y el verso cae al alma como al pasto el rocío.

Qué importa que mi amor no pudiera guardarla.
La noche está estrellada y ella no está conmigo.

Eso es todo. A lo lejos alguien canta. A lo lejos.
Mi alma no se contenta con haberla perdido.

Como para acercarla mi mirada la busca.
Mi corazón la busca, y ella no está conmigo.

La misma noche que hace blanquear los mismos árboles.
Nosotros, los de entonces, ya no somos los mismos.

Ya no la quiero, es cierto, pero cuánto la quise.
Mi voz buscaba el viento para tocar su oído.

De otro. Será de otro. Como antes de mis besos.
Su voz, su cuerpo claro. Sus ojos infinitos.

xx *Tonight I Can Write ...*

Tonight I can write the saddest lines.

Write, for example, 'The night is shattered
and the blue stars shiver in the distance.'

The night wind revolves in the sky and sings.

Tonight I can write the saddest lines.
I loved her, and sometimes she loved me too.

Through nights like this one I held her in my arms.
I kissed her again and again under the endless sky.

She loved me, sometimes I loved her too.
How could one not have loved her great still eyes.

Tonight I can write the saddest lines.
To think that I do not have her. To feel that I have lost her.

To hear the immense night, still more immense without her.
And the verse falls to the soul like dew to the pasture.

What does it matter that my love could not keep her.
The night is shattered and she is not with me.

This is all. In the distance someone is singing. In the distance.
My soul is not satisfied that it has lost her.

My sight searches for her as though to go to her.
My heart looks for her, and she is not with me.

The same night whitening the same trees.
We, of that time, are no longer the same.

I no longer love her, that's certain, but how I loved her.
My voice tried to find the wind to touch her hearing.

Another's. She will be another's. Like my kisses before.
Her voice. Her bright body. Her infinite eyes.

Ya no la quiero, es cierto, pero tal vez la quiero.
Es tan corto el amor, y es tan largo el olvido.

Porque en noches como ésta la tuve entre mis brazos,
mi alma no se contenta con haberla perdido.

Aunque éste sea el último dolor que ella me causa,
y éstos sean los últimos versos que yo le escribo.

I no longer love her, that's certain, but maybe I love her.
Love is so short, forgetting is so long.

Because through nights like this one I held her in my arms
my soul is not satisfied that it has lost her.

Though this be the last pain that she makes me suffer
and these the last verses that I write for her.

[W.S.M.]

from *Residencia en la tierra, I* (1933)

Alianza (Sonata)

De miradas polvorientas caídas al suelo
o de hojas sin sonido y sepultándose.
De metales sin luz, con el vacío,
con la ausencia del día muerto de golpe.
En lo alto de las manos el deslumbrar de mariposas,
el arrancar de mariposas cuya luz no tiene término.

Tú guardabas la estela de luz, de seres rotos
que el sol abandonado, atardeciendo, arroja a las iglesias.
Teñida con miradas, con objeto de abejas,
tu material de inesperada llama huyendo
precede y sigue al día y a su familia de oro.

Los días acechando cruzan en sigilo
pero caen adentro de tu voz de luz.
Oh dueña del amor, en tu descanso
fundé mi sueño, mi actitud callada.

Con tu cuerpo de número tímido, extendido de pronto
hasta las cantidades que definen la tierra,
detrás de la pelea de los días blancos de espacio
y fríos de muertes lentas y estímulos marchitos,
siento arder tu regazo y transitar tus besos
haciendo golondrinas frescas en mi sueño.

A veces el destino de tus lágrimas asciende
como la edad hasta mi frente, allí
están golpeando las olas, destruyéndose de muerte:
su movimiento es húmedo, decaído, final.

Alliance (Sonata)

From dust-laden glances, fallen to earth,
or noiseless leaves, self-buried.
From tarnished metals, with the void incarnate,
with the absence of day, dead of a stroke.
In hand-heights, the dazzle of butterflies,
butterflies setting sail in their unbounded light.

You were guardian to the light's stelae, fragmented beings
the late and tardy sun flung at the churches.
Glance-tinted, with the aim of bees,
your embodiment of unlooked-for flame in flight
precedes and follows day, his golden kin.

Days cruise in secret and lie in ambush
but fall into the trap: your voice of light.
Oh lady of the house of love – in your repose
I ground my dreams, my hushed expectancy.

With your body shyly numbered, extended suddenly
out to the quantities which have defined the earth,
beyond the broils of the white days in space,
cold with slow deaths and withering incentives,
I feel your lap burning and your kisses passing
like early summer swallows in my dreams.

Times are when what your tears may wish to be
like age reaches my forehead –
there waves are battering tripping themselves to death:
their motion humid, fallen, final.

[N.T.]

Débil del alba

El día de los desventurados, el día pálido se asoma
con un desgarrador olor frío, con sus fuerzas en gris,
sin cascabeles, goteando el alba por todas partes:
es un naufragio en el vacío, con un alrededor de llanto.

Porque se fué de tantos sitios la sombra húmeda, callada,
de tantas cavilaciones en vano, de tantos parajes terrestres
en donde debió ocupar hasta el designio de las raíces,
de tanta forma aguda que se defendía.

Yo lloro en medio de lo invadido, entre lo confuso,
entre el sabor creciente, poniendo el oído
en la pura circulación, en el aumento,
cediendo sin rumbo el paso a lo que arriba,
a lo que surge vestido de cadenas y claveles,
yo sueño, sobrellevando mis vestigios morales.

Nada hay de precipitado, ni de alegre, ni de forma orgullosa,
todo aparece haciéndose con evidente pobreza,
la luz de la tierra sale de sus párpados
no como la campanada, sino más bien como las lágrimas:
el tejido del día, su lienzo débil,
sirve para una venda de enfermos, sirve para hacer señas
en una despedida, detrás de la ausencia:
es el color que sólo quiere reemplazar,
cubrir, tragar, vencer, hacer distancias.

Estoy solo entre materias desvencijadas,
la lluvia cae sobre mí, y se me parece,
se me parece con su desvarío, solitaria en el mundo muerto,
rechazada al caer, y sin forma obstinada.

Weak with the Dawn

The day of the luckless, the pale day appears
with a cold heart-breaking smell, with its forces in grey,
with no bells on, dripping dawn from everywhere:
it is a shipwreck in a void, surrounded by weeping.

For the moist shadow went from so many places,
from so many vain objections, from so many earthly halts
where it should have occupied even the design of the roots,
from so much sharp form that defended itself.

I weep in the midst of what is invaded, amid the uncertain,
amid the growing savour, lending the ear
to the pure circulation, to the increase,
without direction giving way to what is approaching,
to what issues forth dressed in chains and carnations,
I dream, burdened with my moral remains.

There is nothing sudden, nor light-hearted, nor with a proud form,
everything seems to be making itself with obvious poverty,
the light of the earth comes out of its eyelids
not like a bell's ringing, but more like tears:
the fabric of the day, its frail linen,
is good for a gauze for the sick, is good for waving
goodbye, in the wake of an absence:
it is the colour that wants only to replace,
to cover, to engulf, to subdue, to make distances.

I am alone with rickety materials,
the rain falls on me, and it is like me,
it is like me in its raving, alone in the dead world,
repulsed as it falls, and with no persistent form.

[W. S. M.]

39

Colección nocturna

He vencido al ángel del sueño, el funesto alegórico:
su gestión insistía, su denso paso llega
envuelto en caracoles y cigarras,
marino, perfumado de frutos agudos.

Es el viento que agita los meses, el silbido de un tren,
el paso de la temperatura sobre el lecho,
un opaco sonido de sombra
que cae como trapo en lo interminable,
una repetición de distancias, un vino de color confundido,
un paso polvoriento de vacas bramando.

A veces su canasto negro cae en mi pecho,
sus sacos de dominio hieren mi hombro,
su multitud de sal, su ejército entreabierto
recorren y revuelven las cosas del cielo:
él galopa en la respiración y su paso es de beso:
su salitre seguro planta en los párpados
con vigor esencial y solemne propósito:
entra en lo preparado como un dueño:
su substancia sin ruido equipa de pronto,
su alimento profético propaga tenazmente.

Reconozco a menudo sus guerreros,
sus piezas corroídas por el aire, sus dimensiones,
y su necesidad de espacio es tan violenta
que baja hasta mi corazón a buscarlo:
él es el propietario de las mesetas inaccesibles,
él baila con personajes trágicos y cotidianos:
de noche rompe mi piel su ácido aéreo
y escucho en mi interior temblar su instrumento.

Yo oigo el sueño de viejos compañeros y mujeres amadas,
sueños cuyos latidos me quebrantan:
su material de alfombra piso en silencio,
su luz de amapola muerdo con delirio.

Cadáveres dormidos que a menudo
danzan asidos al peso de mi corazón

Nocturnal Collection

I have conquered the angel of dream, he of woe and allegory:
his effort was tireless, his packed footstep comes
wrapped in snails and cigars,
marine, perfumed with sharp fruit.

It is the wind that shakes the months, the whistle of a train,
the march of temperature over the bed,
an opaque sound of shadow
falling like a rag where there is no end,
a repetition of distances, a wine of unsettled colour,
a dusty footstep of lowing cows.

Sometimes his black basket falls in my chest,
his sacks of dominion hurt my shoulder,
his multitude of salt, his unlatched army
turn around the things of the sky and make them turn:
he gallops in the breath with the pace of kisses:
he plants his sure saltpetre on the eyelids
with essential vigour and solemn purpose:
he enters into what is prepared like an owner:
he furnishes suddenly his noiseless substance,
stubbornly his prophetic nourishment spreads.

Often I recognize his warriors,
their arms corroded by the air, their dimensions,
and their need of space is so violent
that it descends to my heart itself in search of it:
he is the owner of inaccessible plateaux,
he dances with tragic and ordinary personages,
at night his aerial acid breaks my skin
and I listen to his instrument trembling within me.

I hear the dream of old companions and of beloved women,
dreams whose throbbing shatters me:
silently I tread their carpet substance,
deliriously I close my teeth on their poppy light.

Sleeping cadavers that often
dance, tied to the pace of my heart,

qué ciudades opacas recorremos!
Mi pardo corcel de sombra se agiganta,
y sobre envejecidos tahures, sobre lenocinios de escaleras gastadas,
sobre lechos de niñas desnudas, entre jugadores de foot-ball,
del viento ceñidos pasamos:
y entonces caen a nuestra boca esos frutos blandos del cielo,
los pájaros, las campanas conventuales, los cometas:
aquel que se nutrió de geografía pura y estremecimiento,
ése tal vez nos vió pasar centelleando.

Camaradas cuyas cabezas reposan sobre barriles,
en un desmantelado buque prófugo, lejos,
amigos míos sin lágrimas, mujeres de rostro cruel:
la medianoche ha llegado y un gong de muerte
golpea en torno mío como el mar.
Hay en la boca el sabor, la sal del dormido.

Fiel como una condena, a cada cuerpo
la palidez del distrito letárgico acude:
una sonrisa fría, sumergida,
unos ojos cubiertos como fatigados boxeadores,
una respiración que sordamente devora fantasmas.

En esa humedad de nacimiento, con esa proporción tenebrosa,
cerrada como una bodega, el aire es criminal:
las paredes tienen un triste color de cocodrilo,
una contextura de araña siniestra:
se pisa en lo blando como sobre un monstruo muerto:
las uvas negras inmensas, repletas,
cuelgan de entre las ruinas como odres:
oh Capitán, en nuestra hora de reparto
abre los mudos cerrojos y espérame:
allí debemos cenar vestidos de luto:
el enfermo de malaria guardará las puertas.

Mi corazón, es tarde y sin orillas,
el día, como un pobre mantel puesto a secar,
oscila rodeado de seres y extensión:
de cada ser viviente hay algo en la atmósfera:
mirando mucho el aire aparecerían mendigos,
abogados, bandidos, carteros, costureras,
y un poco de cada oficio, un resto humillado

what opaque cities we are passing through!
My brown horse of shadow grows huge,
and over aged gamblers, over pimps from worn stairs,
over beds of nude girls, among soccer players,
hemmed round by the wind, we pass:
and then those bland fruits of the sky fall to our mouth,
the birds, the convent bells, the comets:
he who nourished himself on pure geography and shuddering
may have seen us go flashing by.

Comrades whose heads rest on barrels,
in a derelict fugitive vessel, far away,
friends of mine without tears, women with cruel faces:
midnight has arrived and a gong of death
beats around me like the sea.
There is a taste in the mouth, the salt of the sleeper.

Faithful as a pronounced sentence, the pallor
of the sluggish district attends each body:
a cold smile, submerged,
eyes swathed like tired boxers,
a breath quietly devouring phantoms.

In that moisture of birth, with that murky occasion,
closed like a cellar, the air is criminal,
the walls have a sad crocodile colour,
a sinister spider's texture:
it is soft underfoot, like a dead monster:
the immense black grapes, full to bursting,
hang among the ruins like wine skins:
oh Captain, in our hour of distribution
open the mute latches and wait for me:
there we are to dine dressed in mourning:
the malaria patient will guard the doors.

My heart, it is late and without shores,
day, like a poor tablecloth put to dry,
sways, surrounded by beings and extent:
there is something from every living being in the atmosphere:
close inspection of the air would disclose beggars,
lawyers, bandits, mailmen, seamstresses,
and a little of each occupation, a humbled remnant

quiere trabajar su parte en nuestro interior.
Yo busco desde antaño, yo examino sin arrogancia,
conquistado, sin duda, por lo vespertino.

wants to perform its own work within us.
I have been searching for a long time, I examine in all modesty,
overcome, without doubt, by evening.

[W.S.M.]

Arte poética

Entre sombra y espacio, entre guarniciones y doncellas,
dotado de corazón singular y sueños funestos,
precipitadamente pálido, marchito en la frente
y con luto de viudo furioso por cada día de vida,
ay, para cada agua invisible que bebo soñolientamente
y de todo sonido que acojo temblando,
tengo la misma sed ausente y la misma fiebre fría
un oído que nace, una angustia indirecta,
como si llegaran ladrones o fantasmas,
y en una cáscara de extensión fija y profunda,
como un camarero humillado, como una campana un poco ronca,
como un espejo viejo, como un olor de casa sola
en la que los huéspedes entran de noche perdidamente ebrios,
y hay un olor de ropa tirada al suelo, y una ausencia de flores
– posiblemente de otro modo aún menos melancólico –,
pero, la verdad, de pronto, el viento que azota mi pecho,
las noches de substancia infinita caídas en mi dormitorio,
el ruido de un día que arde con sacrificio
me piden lo profético que hay en mí, con melancolía
y un golpe de objetos que llaman sin ser respondidos
hay, y un movimiento sin tregua, y un nombre confuso.

Ars Poetica

Between shadow and space, young girls and garrisons,
saddled with a strange heart, with funereal dreams,
taken suddenly pale, my forehead withered
by the rage of a widower's grief for each day of lost life –
oh for each invisible drop I drink in a stupor
and for each sound I harbour, trembling,
I nurse the same far thirst, the same cold fever,
a noise in labour, a devious anguish –
as if thieves or emanations were coming –
in the enveloping shell, rooted, profound,
like a humiliated scullion, a bell cracked a little,
a mirror tarnished, the fug of a deserted house
whose guests come in at night sloshed to perdition,
with a stench of clothes scattered on the floor
and a yearning for flowers –
another way to put it perhaps, a touch less sadly:
but the hard truth is if you want it so,
this wind that whacks at my breast,
the unbounded expanse of night collapsing in my bedroom,
the morning's rumours afire with sacrifice
now beg of me this prophecy I have, with mournfulness
and a lurch of objects calling without answers,
with a truceless movement, a name I can't make out.

[N.T.]

Caballero solo

Los jóvenes homosexuales y las muchachas amorosas,
y las largas viudas que sufren el delirante insomnio,
y las jóvenes señoras preñadas hace treinta horas,
y los roncos gatos que cruzan mi jardín en tinieblas,
como un collar de palpitantes ostras sexuales
rodean mi residencia solitaria,
como enemigos establecidos contra mi alma,
como conspiradores en traje de dormitorio
que cambiaran largos besos espesos por consigna.

El radiante verano conduce a los enamorados
en uniformes regimientos melancólicos,
hechos de gordas y flacas y alegres y tristes parejas:
bajo los elegantes cocoteros, junto al océano y la luna,
hay una continua vida de pantalones y polleras.
un rumor de medias de seda acariciadas,
y senos femeninos que brillan como ojos.

El pequeño empleado, después de mucho,
después del tedio semanal, y las novelas leídas de noche en cama
ha definitivamente seducido a su vecina,
y la lleva a los miserables cinematógrafos
donde los héroes son potros o príncipes apasionados,
y acaricia sus piernas llenas de dulce vello
con sus ardientes y húmedas manos que huelen a cigarrillo.

Los atardeceres del seductor y las noches de los esposos
se unen como dos sábanas sepultándome,
y las horas después del almuerzo en que los jóvenes estudiantes
y las jóvenes estudiantes, y los sacerdotes se masturban,
y los animales fornican directamente,
y las abejas huelen a sangre, y las moscas zumban coléricas,
y los primos juegan extrañamente con sus primas,
y los médicos miran con furia al marido de la joven paciente,
y las horas de la mañana en que el profesor, como por descuido,
cumple con su deber conyugal y desayuna,
y más aún, los adúlteros, que se aman con verdadero amor
sobre lechos altos y largos como embarcaciones:
seguramente, eternamente me rodea

Lone Gentleman

Young homosexuals and girls in love,
and widows gone to seed, sleepless, delirious,
and novice housewives pregnant some thirty hours,
the hoarse cats cruising across my garden's shadows
like a necklace of throbbing, sexual oysters
surround my solitary home
like enemies entrenched against my soul,
like conspirators in pyjamas
exchanging long, thick kisses on the sly.

The radiant summer entices lovers here
in melancholic regiments
made up of fat and flabby, gay and mournful couples:
under the graceful palm trees, along the moonlit beach,
there is a continual excitement of trousers and petticoats,
the crisp sound of stockings caressed,
women's breasts shining like eyes.

It's quite clear that the local clerk, bored to the hilt,
after his weekday tedium, cheap paperbacks in bed,
has managed to make his neighbour
and he takes her to the miserable flea-pits
where the heroes are young stallions or passionate princes:
he caresses her legs downy with soft hair
with his wet, hot hands smelling of cigarillos.

Seducer's afternoons and strictly legal nights
fold together like a pair of sheets, burying me:
the siesta hours when young male and female students
as well as priests retire to masturbate,
and when animals screw outright,
and bees smell of blood and furious flies buzz,
and cousins play kinkily with their girl cousins,
and doctors glare angrily at their young patient's husband,
and the professor, almost unconsciously, during the morning hours,
copes with his marital duties and then has breakfast,
and, later on, the adulterers who love each other with real love,
on beds as high and spacious as sea-going ships –
so for sure and for ever this great forest surrounds me,

este gran bosque respiratorio y enredado
con grandes flores como bocas y dentaduras
y negras raíces en forma de uñas y zapatos.

breathing through flowers large as mouths chock full of teeth,
black-rooted in the shapes of hoofs and shoes.

[N.T.]

Tango del viudo

Oh Maligna, ya habrás hallado la carta, ya habrás llorado de furia,
y habrás insultado el recuerdo de mi madre
llamándola perra podrida y madre de perros,
ya habrás bebido sola, solitaria, el té del atardecer
mirando mis viejos zapatos vacíos para siempre
y ya no podrás recordar mis enfermedades, mis sueños nocturnos, mis comidas,
sin maldecirme en voz alta como si estuviera allí aún
quejándome del trópico de los *coolíes corringhis*,
de las venenosas fiebres que me hicieron tanto daño
y de los espantosos ingleses que odio todavía.

Maligna, la verdad, qué noche tan grande, qué tierra tan sola!
He llegado otra vez a los dormitorios solitarios,
a almorzar en los restaurantes comida fría, y otra vez
tiro al suelo los pantalones y las camisas,
no hay perchas en mi habitación, ni retratos de nadie en las paredes.
Cuánta sombra de la que hay en mi alma daría por recobrarte,
y qué amenazadores me parecen los nombres de los meses,
y la palabra invierno qué sonido de tambor lúgubre tiene.

Enterrado junto al cocotero hallarás más tarde
el cuchillo que escondí allí por temor de que me mataras,
y ahora repentinamente quisiera oler su acero de cocina
acostumbrado al peso de tu mano y al brillo de tu pie:
bajo la humedad de la tierra, entre las sordas raíces,
de los lenguajes humanos el pobre sólo sabría tu nombre,
y la espesa tierra no comprende tu nombre
hecho de impenetrables substancias divinas.

Así como me aflige pensar en el claro día de tus piernas
recostadas como detenidas y duras aguas solares,
y la golondrina que durmiendo y volando vive en tus ojos,
y el perro de furia que asilas en el corazón,
así también veo las muertes que están entre nosotros desde ahora,
y respiro en el aire la ceniza y lo destruido,
el largo, solitario espacio que me rodea para siempre.

Daría este viento del mar gigante por tu brusca respiración
oída en largas noches sin mezcla de olvido,

Widower's Tango

Oh Maligna, by now you will have found the letter, by now you will have cried
    with rage
and you will have insulted the memory of my mother
calling her a rotten bitch and a mother of dogs,
by now you will have drunk alone, all by yourself, your afternoon tea
with your eyes on my old shoes which are empty forever,
and by now you will not be able to recall my illnesses, my dreams at night, my
    meals
without cursing me out loud as though I were still there
complaining of the tropics, of the *coolies corringhis,*
of the poisonous fevers which did me such harm,
and of the horrendous English whom I still hate.

Maligna, the truth of it, how huge the night is, how lonely the earth!
I have gone back again to single bedrooms,
to cold lunches in restaurants, and I
drop my pants and my shirts on the floor as I used to,
there are no hangers in my room, and nobody's pictures are on the walls,
How much of the shadow that is in my soul I would give to have you back,
the names of the months sound to me like threats
and the word winter is like the sound of lugubrious drum.

Later on you will find buried near the coconut tree
the knife which I hid there for fear you would kill me,
and now suddenly I would be glad to smell its kitchen steel
used to the weight of your hand, the shine of your foot:
under the dampness of the ground, among the deaf roots,
in all the languages of men only the poor will know your name,
and the dense earth does not understand your name
made of impenetrable divine substances.

Thus it hurts me to think of the clear day of your legs
in repose like waters of the sun made to stay in place,
and the swallow that lives in your eyes sleeping and flying,
and the mad dog that you harbour in your heart,
and thus also I see the dead who are between us and will be from now on,
and I breathe ash and utter ruin in the air itself,
I would give this giant sea-wind for your sudden breath
and the vast solitary space that will be around me forever.

uniéndose a la atmósfera como el látigo a la piel del caballo.
Y por oírte orinar, en la oscuridad, en el fondo de la casa,
como vertiendo una miel delgada, trémula, argentina, obstinada,
cuántas veces entregaría este coro de sombras que poseo,
y el ruido de espadas inútiles que se oye en mi alma,
y la paloma de sangre que está solitaria en mi frente
llamando cosas desaparecidas, seres desaparecidos,
substancias extrañamente inseparables y perdidas.

I would give this wind off the giant sea for your hoarse breathing
heard in the long nights unmixed with oblivion,
becoming part of the atmosphere as the whip becomes part of the horse's skin.
And to hear you make water, in the darkness, at the bottom of the house,
as though you were pouring a slow, tremulous, silvery, obstinate honey,
how many times over would I yield up this choir of shadows which I possess,
and the clash of useless swords which is audible in my soul,
and the dove of blood, alone on my forehead,
calling to things which have vanished, to beings who have vanished,
to substances incomprehensibly inseparable and lost.

[W.S.M.]

from *Residencia en la tierra, II* (1935)

Sólo la muerte

Hay cementerios solos,
tumbas llenas de huesos sin sonido,
el corazón pasando un túnel
oscuro, oscuro, oscuro,
como un naufragio hacia adentro nos morimos,
como ahogarnos en el corazón,
como irnos cayendo desde la piel al alma.

Hay cadáveres,
hay pies de pegajosa losa fría,
hay la muerte en los huesos,
como un sonido puro,
como un ladrido sin perro,
saliendo de ciertas campanas, de ciertas tumbas,
creciendo en la humedad como el llanto o la lluvia.

Yo veo, solo, a veces,
ataúdes a vela
zarpar con difuntos pálidos, con mujeres de trenzas muertas,
con panaderos blancos como ángeles,
con niñas pensativas casadas con notarios,
ataúdes subiendo el río vertical de los muertos,
el río morado,
hacia arriba, con las velas hinchadas por el sonido de la muerte,
hinchadas por el sonido silencioso de la muerte.

A lo sonoro llega la muerte
como un zapato sin pie, como un traje sin hombre,
llega a golpear con un anillo sin piedra y sin dedo,
llega a gritar sin boca, sin lengua, sin garganta.
Sin embargo sus pasos suenan
y su vestido suena, callado, como un árbol.

Yo no sé, yo conozco poco, yo apenas veo,
pero creo que su canto tiene color de violetas húmedas,
de violetas acostumbradas a la tierra,
porque la cara de la muerte es verde,
y la mirada de la muerte es verde,

Death Alone

There are lone cemeteries,
tombs full of soundless bones,
the heart threading a tunnel,
a dark, dark tunnel:
like a wreck we die to the very core,
as if drowning at the heart
or collapsing inwards from skin to soul.

There are corpses,
clammy slabs for feet,
there is death in the bones,
like a pure sound,
a bark without its dog,
out of certain bells, certain tombs
swelling in this humidity like lament or rain.

I see, when alone at times,
coffins under sail
setting out with the pale dead, women in their dead braids,
bakers as white as angels,
thoughtful girls married to notaries,
coffins ascending the vertical river of the dead,
the wine-dark river to its source,
with their sails swollen with the sound of death,
filled with the silent noise of death.

Death is drawn to sound
like a slipper without a foot, a suit without its wearer,
comes to knock with a ring, stoneless and fingerless,
comes to shout without a mouth, a tongue, without a throat.
Nevertheless its footsteps sound
and its clothes echo, hushed like a tree.

I do not know, I am ignorant, I hardly see
but it seems to me that its song has the colour of wet violets,
violets well used to the earth,
since the face of death is green,
and the gaze of death green

con la aguda humedad de una hoja de violeta
y su grave color de invierno exasperado.

Pero la muerte va también por el mundo vestida de escoba,
lame el suelo buscando difuntos,
la muerte está en la escoba,
es la lengua de la muerte buscando muertos,
es la aguja de la muerte buscando hilo.

La muerte está en los catres:
en los colchones lentos, en las frazadas negras
vive tendida, y de repente sopla:
sopla un sonido oscuro que hincha sábanas,
y hay camas navegando a un puerto
en donde está esperando, vestida de almirante.

with the etched moisture of a violet's leaf
and its grave colour of exasperated winter.

But death goes about the earth also, riding a broom
lapping the ground in search of the dead –
death is in the broom,
it is the tongue of death looking for the dead,
the needle of death looking for thread.

Death lies in our cots:
in the lazy mattresses, the black blankets,
lives at full stretch and then suddenly blows,
blows sound unknown filling out the sheets
and there are beds sailing into a harbour
where death is waiting, dressed as an admiral.

[N.T.]

Barcarola

Si solamente me tocaras el corazón,
si solamente pusieras tu boca en mi corazón,
tu fina boca, tus dientes,
si pusieras tu lengua como una flecha roja
allí donde mi corazón polvoriento golpea,
si soplaras en mi corazón, cerca del mar, llorando,
sonaría con un ruido oscuro, con sonido de ruedas de tren con sueño,
como aguas vacilantes,
como el otoño en hojas,
como sangre,
con un ruido de llamas húmedas quemando el cielo,
sonando como sueños o ramas o lluvias,
o bocinas de puerto triste,
si tú soplaras en mi corazón cerca del mar,
como un fantasma blanco,
al borde de la espuma,
en mitad del viento,
como un fantasma desencadenado, a la orilla del mar, llorando.

Como ausencia extendida, como campana súbita,
el mar reparte el sonido del corazón,
lloviendo, atardeciendo, en una costa sola:
la noche cae sin duda,
y su lúgubre azul de estandarte en naufragio
se puebla de planetas de plata enronquecida.

Y suena el corazón como un caracol agrio,
llama, oh mar, oh lamento, oh derretido espanto
esparcido en desgracias y olas desvencijadas:
de lo sonoro el mar acusa
sus sombras recostadas, sus amapolas verdes.

Si existieras de pronto, en una costa lúgubre,
rodeada por el día muerto,
frente a una nueva noche,
llena de olas,
y soplaras en mi corazón de miedo frío,
soplaras en la sangre sola de mi corazón,
soplaras en su movimiento de paloma con llamas,

Barcarole

If only you would touch my heart,
if only you would put your lips to my heart,
your delicate mouth, your teeth,
if you would place your tongue like a red arrow
where my crumbling heart is beating,
if you would blow over my heart, near the sea, crying,
it would ring with an obscure sound, the sound of train wheels, of dreams,
like the to and fro of waters,
like autumn in leaf,
like blood,
with a noise of damp flames burning the sky,
dreaming like dreams, or branches, or winds,
or the horns of some sad port,
if you would blow on my heart near the sea
like a white ghost would blow,
on the lace of the spume,
in the cut of the wind,
like an unchained ghost crying at the sea's edge.

Like absence spun out, like a sudden bell,
the sea shares out the heart's own sound,
raining, dusking on a lone coast:
night falls without doubts
and the lugubrious blue of its shipwrecked banners
fills with a stridency of silver planets.

And the heart sounds like a crabbed shell,
calls: oh sea, oh cry, oh fear dissolved,
scattered in wreckages and dislocated waves:
the sea impeaches sound
for its leaning shadows, its green poppies.

If you were to come into being suddenly, on some sad coast,
surrounded by the stuff of the dead day,
face to face with a new night,
full of waves,
and were to blow on my cold, fearful heart,
on its lonesome blood,
on its flames like a flight of doves,

sonarían sus negras sílabas de sangre,
crecerían sus incesantes aguas rojas,
y sonaría, sonaría a sombras,
sonaría como la muerte,
llamaría como un tubo lleno de viento o llanto,
o una botella echando espanto a borbotones.

Así es, y los relámpagos cubrirían tus trenzas
y la lluvia entraría por tus ojos abiertos
a preparar el llanto que sordamente encierras,
y las alas negras del mar girarían en torno
de ti, con grandes garras, y graznidos, y vuelos.

Quieres ser el fantasma que sople, solitario,
cerca del mar su estéril, triste instrumento?
Si solamente llamaras,
su prolongado son, su maléfico pito,
su orden de olas heridas,
alguien vendría acaso,
alguien vendría,
desde las cimas de las islas, desde el fondo rojo del mar,
alguien vendría, alguien vendría.

Alguien vendría, sopla con furia,
que suene como sirena de barco roto,
como lamento,
como un relincho en medio de la espuma y la sangre,
como un agua feroz mordiéndose y sonando.

En la estación marina
su caracol de sombra circula como un grito,
los pájaros del mar lo desestiman y huyen,
sus listas de sonido, sus lúgubres barrotes
se levantan a orillas del océano solo.

its black blood syllables would sound,
its unquenchable red waters swell
and it would sound and sound in the shadows,
it would sound like death itself,
calling like a pipe full of wind and crying,
or a bottle gushing fright.

So it is, and lightning would glaze your tresses,
and rain would come in through your open eyes
to hatch the cry you have incubated here
and the black wings of the sea would whirl round you
with a great flail of talons and raven cawings.

Do you want to be the lone ghost by the sea
blowing his pointless, disheartened instrument?
If only you would call
his drawn-out sound, his evil piping,
his melody of wounded waves,
someone would come perhaps,
someone would come,
from the crowns of the islands, up from the red sea depths
someone would come, someone indeed would come.

Someone would come, blow with fury,
that it may sound like the siren of a broken ship,
like a lament,
like neighing from the midst of surf and blood,
like fierce and self-devouring waters.

In the marine season
a shell of shadows spirals like a cry,
seabirds mistrust it and flee,
its shreds of sound, its grid of misery
rise by the shores of the solitary ocean.

[N.T.]

Walking Around

Sucede que me canso de ser hombre.
Sucede que entro en las sastrerías y en los cines
marchito, impenetrable, como un cisne de fieltro
navegando en un agua de origen y ceniza.

El olor de las peluquerías me hace llorar a gritos.
Sólo quiero un descanso de piedras o de lana,
sólo quiero no ver establecimientos ni jardines,
ni mercaderías, ni anteojos, ni ascensores.

Sucede que me canso de mis pies y mis uñas
y mi pelo y mi sombra.
Sucede que me canso de ser hombre.

Sin embargo sería delicioso
asustar a un notario con un lirio cortado
o dar muerte a una monja con un golpe de oreja.
Sería bello
ir por las calles con un cuchillo verde
y dando gritos hasta morir de frío.

No quiero seguir siendo raíz en las tinieblas,
vacilante, extendido, tiritando de sueño,
hacia abajo, en las tapias mojadas de la tierra,
absorbiendo y pensando, comiendo cada día.

No quiero para mí tantas desgracias.
No quiero continuar de raíz y de tumba,
de subterráneo solo, de bodega con muertos
ateridos, muriéndome de pena.

Por eso el día lunes arde como el petróleo
cuando me ve llegar con mi cara de cárcel,
y aúlla en su transcurso como una rueda herida,
y da pasos de sangre caliente hacia la noche.

Y me empuja a ciertos rincones, a ciertas casas húmedas,
a hospitales donde los huesos salen por la ventana,

Walking Around

It happens that I am tired of being a man.
It happens that I go into the tailor's shops and the movies
all shrivelled up, impenetrable, like a felt swan
navigating on a water of origin and ash.

The smell of barber shops makes me sob out loud.
I want nothing but the repose either of stones or of wool,
I want to see no more establishments, no more gardens,
nor merchandise, nor glasses, nor elevators.

It happens that I am tired of my feet and my nails
and my hair and my shadow.
It happens that I am tired of being a man.

Just the same it would be delicious
to scare a notary with a cut lily
or knock a nun stone dead with one blow of an ear.
It would be beautiful
to go through the streets with a green knife
shouting until I died of cold.

I do not want to go on being a root in the dark,
hesitating, stretched out, shivering with dreams,
downwards, in the wet tripe of the earth,
soaking it up and thinking, eating every day.

I do not want to be the inheritor of so many misfortunes.
I do not want to continue as a root and as a tomb,
as a solitary tunnel, as a cellar full of corpses,
stiff with cold, dying with pain.

For this reason Monday burns like oil
at the sight of me arriving with my jail-face,
and it howls in passing like a wounded wheel,
and its footsteps towards nightfall are filled with hot blood.

And it shoves me along to certain corners, to certain damp houses,
to hospitals where the bones come out of the windows,

a ciertas zapaterías con olor a vinagre,
a calles espantosas como grietas.

Hay pájaros de color de azufre y horribles intestinos
colgando de las puertas de las casas que odio,
hay dentaduras olvidadas en una cafetera,
hay espejos
que debieran haber llorado de vergüenza y espanto,
hay paraguas en todas partes, y venenos, y ombligos.

Yo paseo con calma, con ojos, con zapatos,
con furia, con olvido,
paso, cruzo oficinas y tiendas de ortopedia,
y patios donde hay ropas colgadas de un alambre:
calzoncillos, toallas y camisas que lloran
lentas lágrimas sucias.

to certain cobblers' shops smelling of vinegar,
to streets horrendous as crevices.

There are birds the colour of sulphur, and horrible intestines
hanging from the doors of the houses which I hate,
there are forgotten sets of teeth in a coffee-pot,
there are mirrors
which should have wept with shame and horror,
there are umbrellas all over the place, and poisons, and navels.

I stride along with calm, with eyes, with shoes,
with fury, with forgetfulness,
I pass, I cross offices and stores full of orthopaedic appliances,
and courtyards hung with clothes on wires,
underpants, towels and shirts which weep
slow dirty tears.

[W. S. M.]

Oda con un lamento

Oh niña entre las rosas, oh presión de palomas,
oh presidio de peces y rosales,
tu alma es una botella llena de sal sedienta
y una campana llena de uvas es tu piel.

Por desgracia no tengo para darte sino uñas
o pestañas, o pianos derretidos,
o sueños que salen de mi corazón a borbotones,
polvorientos sueños que corren como jinetes negros,
sueños llenos de velocidades y desgracias.

Sólo puedo quererte con besos y amapolas,
con guirnaldas mojadas por la lluvia,
mirando cenicientos caballos y perros amarillos.
Sólo puedo quererte con olas a la espalda,
entre vagos golpes de azufre y aguas ensimismadas,
nadando en contra de los cementerios que corren en ciertos ríos
con pasto mojado creciendo sobre las tristes tumbas de yeso,
nadando a través de corazones sumergidos
y pálidas planillas de niños insepultos.

Hay mucha muerte, muchos acontecimientos funerarios
en mis desamparadas pasiones y desolados besos,
hay el agua que cae en mi cabeza,
mientras crece mi pelo,
un agua como el tiempo, un agua negra desencadenada,
con una voz nocturna, con un grito
de pájaro en la lluvia, con una interminable
sombra de ala mojada que protege mis huesos:
mientras me visto, mientras
interminablemente me miro en los espejos y en los vidrios,
oigo que alguien me sigue llamándome a sollozos
con una triste voz podrida por el tiempo.

Tú estás de pie sobre la tierra, llena
de dientes y relámpagos.
Tú propagas los besos y matas las hormigas.
Tú lloras de salud, de cebolla, de abeja,
de abecedario ardiendo.

Ode with a Lament

Oh girl among the roses, oh pressure of doves,
oh jail of fish and rose-bushes,
your soul is a bottle full of thirsting salt
and a bell of grapes is your skin.

What a pity that I have nothing to give you except
the nails of my fingers, or eyelashes, or pianos melted by love,
or dreams which pour from my heart in torrents,
dreams covered with dust, which gallop like black riders,
dreams full of velocities and misfortunes.

I can love you only with kisses and poppies,
with garlands wet with rain,
my eyes full of ember-red horses and yellow dogs.
I can love you only with waves on the shoulder,
amid random blows of sulphur, and waters lost in thought,
swimming against the cemeteries which run in certain rivers
with wet grass growing over the sad plaster tombs,
swimming across the sunken hearts
and the small pale pages of unburied children.

There is a great deal of death, there are funeral events
in my helpless passions and desolate kisses,
there is the water which falls in my head,
while my hair grows,
a water like time, a black unchained water,
with a nocturnal voice, with the cry
of a bird in the rain, with an unending
shadow, a shadow of a wet wing which protects my bones:
while I dress myself, while
endlessly I stare at myself in the mirrors and window-panes,
I hear someone following me, calling me, sobbing,
with a sad voice rotted by time.

You are standing over the earth, full
of teeth and lightning.
You propagate kisses and you kill the ants.
You weep tears of health, of the onion, of the bee,
of the burning alphabet.

Tú eres como una espada azul y verde
y ondulas al tocarte, como un río.

Ven a mi alma vestida de blanco, con un ramo
de ensangrentadas rosas y copas de cenizas,
ven con una manzana y un caballo,
porque allí hay una sala oscura y un candelabro roto,
unas sillas torcidas que esperan el invierno,
y una paloma muerta, con un número.

You are like a sword, blue and green,
and you undulate to the touch like a river.

Come to my soul dressed in white, with a branch
of bleeding roses and goblets of ashes,
come with an apple and a horse,
for there is a dark room with a broken candelabra,
a few twisted chairs waiting for winter,
and a dead dove, with a number.

[W.S.M.]

No hay olvido (Sonata)

Si me preguntáis en dónde he estado
debo decir 'Sucede'.
Debo de hablar del suelo que oscurecen las piedras,
del río que durando se destruye:
no sé sino las cosas que los pájaros pierden,
el mar dejado atrás, o mi hermana llorando.
Por qué tantas regiones, por qué un día
se junta con un día? Por qué una negra noche
se acumula en la boca? Por qué muertos?

Si me preguntáis de dónde vengo, tengo que conversar con cosas rotas,
con utensilios demasiado amargos,
con grandes bestias a menudo podridas
y con mi acongojado corazón.

No son recuerdos los que se han cruzado
ni es la paloma amarillenta que duerme en el olvido,
sino caras con lágrimas,
dedos en la garganta,
y lo que se desploma de las hojas:
la oscuridad de un día transcurrido,
de un día alimentado con nuestra triste sangre.

He aquí violetas, golondrinas,
todo cuanto nos gusta y aparece
en las dulces tarjetas de larga cola
por donde se pasean el tiempo y la dulzura.

Pero no penetremos más allá de esos dientes,
no mordamos las cáscaras que el silencio acumula,
porque no sé qué contestar:
hay tantos muertos,
y tantos malecones que el sol rojo partía,
y tantas cabezas que golpean los buques,
y tantas manos que han encerrado besos,
y tantas cosas que quiero olvidar.

There's No Forgetting (Sonata)

If you should ask me where I've been all this time
I have to say 'Things happen.'
I have to dwell on stones darkening the earth,
on the river ruined in its own duration:
I know nothing save things the birds have lost,
the sea I left behind, or my sister crying.
Why this abundance of places? Why does day lock
with day? Why the dark night swilling round
in our mouths? And why the dead?

Should you ask me where I come from, I must talk
with broken things,
with fairly painful utensils,
with great beasts turned to dust as often as not
and my afflicted heart.

These are not memories that have passed each other
nor the yellowing pigeon asleep in our forgetting;
these are tearful faces
and fingers down our throats
and whatever among leaves falls to the ground:
the dark of a day gone by
grown fat on our grieving blood.

Here are violets, and here swallows,
all things we love and which inform
sweet messages seriatim
through which time passes and sweetness passes.

We don't get far, though, beyond these teeth:
Why waste time gnawing the husks of silence?
I know not what to answer:
there are so many dead,
and so many dikes the red sun breached,
and so many heads battering hulls
and so many hands that have closed over kisses
and so many things that I want to forget.

[N.T.]

75

from *Tercera Residencia* (1947)

Alianza (Sonata)

Ni el corazón cortado por un vidrio
en un erial de espinas,
ni las aguas atroces vistas en los rincones
de ciertas casas, aguas como párpados y ojos,
podrían sujetar tu cintura en mis manos
cuando mi corazón levanta sus encinas
hacia tu inquebrantable hilo de nieve.

Nocturno azúcar, espíritu
de las coronas,
              redimida
sangre humana, tus besos
me destierran
y un golpe de agua con restos del mar
golpea los silencios que te esperan
rodeando las gastadas sillas, gastando puertas.

Noches con ejes claros,
partida, material, únicamente
voz, únicamente
desnuda cada día.

Sobre tus pechos de corriente inmóvil,
sobre tus piernas de dureza y agua,
sobre la permanencia y el orgullo
de tu pelo desnudo,
quiero estar, amor mío, ya tiradas las lágrimas
al ronco cesto donde se acumulan,
quiero estar, amor mío, solo con una sílaba
de plata destrozada, solo con una punta
de tu pecho de nieve.

Ya no es posible, a veces,
ganar sino cayendo,
ya no es posible, entre dos seres
temblar, tocar la flor del río:
hebras de hombres vienen como agujas,
tramitaciones, trozos,
familias de coral repulsivo, tormentas

Pact (Sonata)

Neither the heart cut by a piece of glass
in a wasteland of thorns
nor the atrocious waters seen in the corners
of certain houses, waters like eyelids and eyes
can capture your waist in my hands
when my heart lifts its oaks
towards your unbreakable thread of snow.

Nocturnal sugar, spirit
of the crowns,
            ransomed
human blood, your kisses
send me into exile
and a stroke of water, with remnants of the sea,
beats on the silences that wait for you
surrounding the worn chairs, wearing out doors.

Nights with bright spindles,
divided, material, nothing
but voice, nothing but
naked every day.

Over your breasts of motionless current,
over your legs of firmness and water,
over the permanence and the pride
of your naked hair
I want to be, my love, now that the tears are thrown
into the raucous basket where they accumulate,
I want to be, my love, alone with a syllable
of mangled silver, alone with a tip
of your breast of snow.

By now sometimes it is not possible
to win except by falling,
by now it is not possible to tremble between
two beings, to touch the flower of the river:
fibres of man come like needles,
procedures, fragments,
families of repulsive coral, torments

y pasos duros por alfombras
de invierno.

Entre labios y labios hay ciudades
de gran ceniza y húmeda cimera,
gotas de cuándo y cómo, indefinidas
circulaciones:
entre labios y labios como por una costa
de arena y vidrio, pasa el viento.

Por eso eres sin fin, recógeme como si fueras
toda solemnidad, toda nocturna
como una zona, hasta que te confundas
con las líneas del tiempo.

                      Avanza en la dulzura,
ven a mi lado hasta que las digitales
hojas de los violines
hayan callado, hasta que los musgos
arraiguen en el trueno, hasta que del latido
de mano y mano bajen las raíces.

and hard steps for winter
carpets.

Between lips and lips there are cities
of great ash and moist summit,
drops of when and how, vague
comings and goings:
between lips and lips as along a shore
of sand and glass the wind passes.

Therefore you are endless; gather me as though you were
all solemnity, all made of night
like a zone, until you are indistinguishable
from the lines of time.

                Advance into sweetness,
come to my side until the fingery
leaves of the violins
have gone silent, until the mosses
take root in the thunder, until from the pulse
of hand and hand the roots descend.

                            [W.S.M.]

Vals

Yo toco el odio como pecho diurno,
yo sin cesar, de ropa en ropa vengo
durmiendo lejos.

No soy, no sirvo, no conozco a nadie,
no tengo armas de mar ni de madera,
no vivo en esta casa.

De noche y agua está mi boca llena.
La duradera luna determina
lo que no tengo.

Lo que tengo está en medio de las olas.
Un rayo de agua, un día para mí:
un fondo férreo.

No hay contramar, no hay escudo, no hay traje,
no hay especial solución insondable,
ni párpado vicioso.

Vivo de pronto y otras veces sigo.
Toco de pronto un rostro y me asesina.
No tengo tiempo.

No me busquéis entonces descorriendo
el habitual hilo salvaje o la
sangrienta enredadera.

No me llaméis: mi ocupación es ésa.
No preguntéis mi nombre ni mi estado.
Dejadme en medio de mi propia luna,
en mi terreno herido.

Waltz

I touch hatred like a covered breast;
I without ceasing come from garment to garment,
sleeping at a distance.

I am not, I'm of no use, I do not know
anyone; I have no weapons of ocean or wood,
I do not live in this house.

My mouth is full of night and water.
The abiding moon determines
what I do not have.

What I have is in the midst of the waves.
A ray of water, a day for myself,
an iron depth.

There is no cross-tide, there is no shield and no costume,
there is no special solution too deep to be sounded,
no vicious eyelid.

I live suddenly and other times I follow.
I touch a face suddenly and it murders me.
I have no time.

Do not look for me then drawing
the usual wild thread or the
bleeding net.

Do not call me: that is my occupation.
Do not ask my name or my condition.
Leave me in the middle of my own moon
in my wounded ground.

[W.S.M.]

Bruselas

De todo lo que he hecho, de todo lo que he perdido,
de todo lo que he ganado sobresaltadamente,
en hierro amargo, en hojas, puedo ofrecer un poco.

Un sabor asustado, un río que las plumas
de las quemantes águilas van cubriendo, un sulfúrico
retroceso de pétalos.

                 No me perdona ya la sal entera
ni el pan continuo, ni la pequeña iglesia devorada
por la lluvia marina, ni el carbón mordido
por la espuma secreta.

He buscado y hallado, pesadamente,
bajo la tierra, entre los cuerpos temibles,
como un diente de pálida madera
llegando y yendo bajo el ácido duro,
junto a los materiales
de la agonía, entre luna y cuchillos,
muriendo de nocturno.

                 Ahora, en medio
de la velocidad desestimada, al lado
de los muros sin hilos,
en el fondo cortado por los términos,
aquí estoy con aquello que pierde estrellas,
vegetalmente, solo.

Brussels: Jeweller's Pincers in Cupellation*

Of all I've done, of all I've lost,
of all I've surprisingly won
in acrid iron, in bitter foil, I can proffer so little:

A taste of fright, a river the feathers
of burning eagles are beginning to smother, a sulphurous
rout of petals.

        I am no longer absolved by ritual salt,
nor reprieved by daily bread, nor by the small church rent
by sea rain, nor cinders splashed
by secret spray.

I have sought and found, weighted down,
under the ground, between fearsome bodies,
like a pale-wood tooth
coming and going under hard acid,
alongside elements
of a death-rattle, between knives and mirror,
nocturnal dying.

        Now, in the midst
of unused speed, beside
wire-less walls,
at the back and bottom, bisected by limits,
here I am with whatever shipwrecks stars,
vegetably, alone.

[A.K.]

* Cupellation: Refinement of gold or silver in a cupel, by exposure to high temperature in a blast of air, by which lead, copper, tin are oxidized and sink into the porous cupel. *Bruselas,* in Spanish, is both the name of the city and of the jeweller's pincers (translators's note).

Naciendo en los bosques

Cuando el arroz retira de la tierra
los granos de su harina,
cuando el trigo endurece sus pequeñas caderas y levanta su rostro de mil manos,
a la enramada donde la mujer y el hombre se enlazan acudo,
para tocar el mar innumerable
de lo que continúa.

Yo no soy hermano del utensilio llevado en la marea
como en una cuna de nácar combatido:
no tiemblo en la comarca de los agonizantes despojos,
no despierto en el golpe de las tinieblas asustadas
por el ronco pecíolo de la campana repentina,
no puede ser, no soy el pasajero
bajo cuyos zapatos los últimos reductos del viento palpitan
y rígidas retornan las olas del tiempo a morir.

Llevo en mi mano la paloma que duerme reclinada en la semilla
y en su fermento espeso de cal y sangre
vive Agosto,
vive el mes extraído de su copa profunda:
con mi mano rodeo la nueva sombra del ala que crece:
la raíz y la pluma que mañana formarán la espesura.

Nunca declina, ni junto al balcón de manos de hierro
ni en el invierno marítimo de los abandonados, ni en mi paso tardío,
el crecimiento inmenso de la gota, ni el párpado que quiere ser abierto:
porque para nacer he nacido, para encerrar el paso
de cuanto se aproxima, de cuanto a mi pecho golpea como un nuevo corazón
   tembloroso.

Vidas recostadas junto a mi traje como palomas paralelas,
o contenidas en mi propia existencia y en mi desordenado sonido
para volver a ser, para incautar el aire desnudo de la hoja
y el nacimiento húmedo de la tierra en la guirnalda: hasta cuándo
debo volver y ser, hasta cuándo el olor
de las más enterradas flores, de las olas más trituradas
sobre las altas piedras, guardan en mí su patria
para volver a ser furia y perfume?

Being Born in the Woods

When the rice withdraws from the earth
the grains of its flour,
when the wheat hardens its little hip-joints and lifts its face of a thousand hands,
I make my way to the grove where the woman and the man embrace,
to touch the innumerable sea
of what continues.

I am not a brother of the implement carried on the tide
as in a cradle of embattled mother-of-pearl:
I do not tremble in the territory of the dying garbage,
I do not wake at the shock of the dark
that is frightened by the hoarse leaf-stalks of the sudden bell,
I cannot be, I am not the traveller
under whose shoes the last remnants of the wind throb
and the waves come back rigid out of time to die.

I carry in my hand the dove that sleeps recumbent in the seed
and in its dense ferment of lime and blood
August lives,
raised out of its deep goblet the month lives:
with my hand I encircle the new shadow of the wing that is growing:
the root and the feather that will form the thicket of tomorrow.

The immense growth of the drop, and the eyelid yearning to be open
never diminish, neither beside the balcony of iron hands
nor in the maritime winter of the abandoned, nor in my late footstep:
for I was born in order to be born, to contain the steps
of all that approaches, of all that beats on my breast like a new trembling heart.

Lives resting beside my clothes like parallel doves
or contained in my own existence and in my lawless sound
in order to return to being, to lay hold on the air denuded of its leaf
and on the moist birth of the soil in the wreath: how long
can I return and be, how long can the odour
of the most deeply buried flowers, of the waves most finely
pulverized on the high rocks, preserve in me their homeland
where they can return to be fury and perfume?

Hasta cuándo la mano del bosque en la lluvia
me avecina con todas sus agujas
para tejer los altos besos del follaje?
                                    Otra vez
escucho aproximarse como el fuego en el humo,
nacer de la ceniza terrestre,
la luz llena de pétalos,
                            y apartando la tierra
en un río de espigas llega el sol a mi boca
como una vieja lágrima enterrada que vuelve a ser semilla.

How long will the hand of the woods in the rain
come close to me with all its needles
to weave the high kisses of the foliage?
                                        Again
I listen to the approach, like that of a fire in smoke,
of the birth of the light full of petals
from the ash of earth,
                              and dividing the ground
into a river of wheat ears the sun reaches my mouth
like an old buried tear that has become seed again.

                                                    [w. s. m.]

(En 1934 fue escrito este poema. Cuántas cosas han sobrevenido desde entonces! España, donde lo escribí, es una cintura de ruinas. Ay! si con sólo una gota de poesía o de amor pudiéramos aplacar la ira del mundo, pero eso sólo lo pueden la lucha y el corazón resuelto.

El mundo ha cambiado y mi poesía ha cambiado. Una gota de sangre caída en estas líneas quedará viviendo sobre ellas, indeleble como el amor.

Marzo de 1939)

Las furias y las penas

'... Hay en mi corazón furias y penas ...'

QUEVEDO

En el fondo del pecho estamos juntos,
en el cañaveral del pecho recorremos
un verano de tigres,
al acecho de un metro de piel fría,
al acecho de un ramo de inaccesible cutis,
con la boca olfateando sudor y venas verdes
nos encontramos en la húmeda sombra que deja caer besos.

Tú mi enemiga de tanto sueño roto de la misma manera
que erizadas plantas de vidrio, lo mismo que campanas
deshechas de manera amenazante, tanto como disparos
de hiedra negra en medio del perfume,
enemiga de grandes caderas que mi pelo han tocado
con un ronco rocío, con una lengua de agua,
no obstante el mudo frío de los dientes y el odio de los ojos,
y la batalla de agonizantes bestias que cuidan el olvido,
en algún sitio del verano estamos juntos
acechando con labios que la sed ha invadido.
Si hay alguien que traspasa
una pared con círculos de fósforo
y hiere el centro de unos dulces miembros
y muerde cada hoja de un bosque dando gritos,
tengo también tus ojos de sangrienta luciérnaga
capaces de impregnar y atravesar rodillas
y gargantas rodeadas de seda general.

Cuando en las reuniones
el azar, la ceniza, las bebidas,

(This poem was written in 1934. How much has happened since then! Spain, where I wrote it, is a belt of ruins. Ah! if we could only placate the world's rage with a drop of poetry or of love – but only the struggle and the daring heart are capable of that.

The world and my poetry have both changed. A drop of blood fallen on these lines will remain alive within them, as indelible as love.

March 1939)

Furies and Sufferings

'. . . There are in my heart furies and sufferings . . .'

QUEVEDO

In the pit of our breasts we are together,
in the heart's plantations we traverse
a summer of tigers.
Lying in wait for a length of cold skin,
a sliver of untouchable complexion,
with our mouths inhaling sweat, with green veins
we meet in the damp shadows, in a rain of kisses.

You my enemy of so much sleep broken in the same manner
as bristling plants of glass, the same as threatening,
dissipated chimes, much like explosions
of black ivy in the distillation of perfume,
my wide-hipped enemy whom my hair has brushed
with an acrid dew, with a tongue of water –
notwithstanding the cold silence of teeth, the hatred of eyes,
the struggle of dying beasts, guardians of oblivion –
in some location of summer we are together
lying in wait with parched lips, possessed by thirst.
If there be anyone who can jump through
a wall with rings of phosphorus
to wound the core of some sweet limbs
biting each leaf of a coppice, shrieking the while,
I also have your eyes of bleeding fireflies
that can fill up and pierce through knees
and throats wreathed in common silk.

When we're at parties –
lady luck, ashes, drinks,

el aire interrumpido,
pero ahí están tus ojos oliendo a cacería,
a rayo verde que agujerea pechos,
tus dientes que abren manzanas de las que cae sangre,
tus piernas que se adhieren al sol dando gemidos,
y tus tetas de nácar y tus pies de amapola,
como embudos llenos de dientes que buscan sombra,
como rosas hechas de látigo y perfume, y aun,
aun más, aun más,
aun detrás de los párpados, aun detrás del cielo,
aun detrás de los trajes y los viajes, en las calles donde la gente orina,
adivinas los cuerpos,
en las agrias iglesias a medio destruir, en las cabinas que el mar lleva en las manos,
acechas con tus labios sin embargo floridos,
rompes a cuchilladas la madera y la plata,
crecen tus grandes venas que asustan:
no hay cáscara, no hay distancia ni hierro,
tocan manos tus manos,
y caes haciendo crepitar las flores negras.

Adivinas los cuerpos!
Como un insecto herido de mandatos,
adivinas el centro de la sangre y vigilas
los músculos que postergan la aurora, asaltas sacudidas,
relámpagos, cabezas,
y tocas largamente las piernas que te guían.

Oh conducida herida de flechas especiales!

Hueles lo húmedo en medio de la noche?

O un brusco vaso de rosales quemados?

Oyes caer la ropa, las llaves, las monedas
en las espesas casas donde llegas desnuda?

Mi odio es una sola mano que te indica
el callado camino, las sábanas en que alguien ha dormido
con sobresalto: llegas
y ruedas por el suelo manejada y mordida,
y el viejo olor del semen como una enredadera
de cenicienta harina se desliza a tu boca.

the staccato air –
but there are your eyes prying, hunting,
green-rayed, puncturing breasts,
your teeth opening apples which drip with blood,
your legs moaning and clasping the sun,
your mother-of-pearl nipples, your poppy feet
like rows of teeth in a funnel looking for shade,
like roses made of whips and perfume, and yet,
yet more, yet more,
even behind eyelids, behind sky,
behind clothes, beyond travels, in the piss-drenched streets,
you divine the bodies,
in the sour, half-ruined churches, in hovels on the sea's hands,
you lie in wait with your lips in flower nonetheless,
gashing wood and silver,
your great veins swell and terrify:
there is no husk, no distance, nor iron,
your hands touch hands
and you fall in fireworks of black flowers.

You smell out bodies!
Like an insect wounded with injunctions
you divine the mid-current of the blood,
watch over muscles holding back the dawn,
storm-strikes, thunders, heads,
and stroke with long caresses the legs that guide you.

Oh channelled wound of specific arrows!

Can you smell out the damp at deep midnight?

Or a rough tub of charred rose-bushes?

Do you hear clothes fall, and keys, and coins
in the thick houses you visit nude?

My hate is but a hand that points towards
hushed streets, the sheets in which someone has slept
in apprehension: you arrive
and tumble on the ground, covered, handled, bitten,
and the old stink of semen like a climbing vine
the shade of ashen flour slithers over your mouth.

Ay leves locas copas y pestañas,
aire que inunda un entreabierto río
como una sola paloma de colérico cauce,
como atributo de agua sublevada,
ay substancias, sabores, párpados de ala viva
con un temblor, con una ciega flor temible,
ay graves, serios pechos como rostros,
ay grandes muslos llenos de miel verde,
y talones y sombra de pies, y transcurridas
respiraciones y superficies de pálida piedra,
y duras olas que suben la piel hacia la muerte
llenas de celestiales harinas empapadas.
Entonces, este río
va entre nosotros, y por una ribera
vas tú mordiendo bocas?

Entonces es que estoy verdaderamente, verdaderamente lejos
y un río de agua ardiendo pasa en lo oscuro?
Ay cuántas veces eres la que el odio no nombra,
y de qué modo hundido en las tinieblas,
y bajo qué lluvias de estiércol machacado
tu estatua en mi corazón devora el trébol.

El odio es un martillo que golpea tu traje
y tu frente escarlata,
y los días del corazón caen en tus orejas
como vagos búhos de sangre eliminada,
y los collares que gota a gota se formaron con lágrimas
rodean tu garganta quemándote la voz como con hielo.

Es para que nunca, nunca
hables, es para que nunca, nunca
salga una golondrina del nido de la lengua
y para que las ortigas destruyan tu garganta
y un viento de buque áspero te habite.

En dónde te desvistes?
En un ferrocarril, junto a un peruano rojo
o con un segador, entre terrones, a la violenta
luz del trigo?
O corres con ciertos abogados de mirada terrible
largamente desnuda, a la orilla del agua de la noche?

Ah light and lunatic foliage and fringes,
air in which an open river drowns
like a sundove in an angry ditch,
like the attributes of rebellious waters,
ah substances, tastes, live-winged eyelids,
trembling with a blind, redoubtable flower,
ah grave and dignified breasts like faces,
great thighs brimming with green honey,
heels and shadows of feet and breathing
lapsed, and tables of pale stone,
and hard waves scaling the skin as far as death
full of a saturation of celestial flour!
And so this river
this river runs between us, and along one bank
do you run biting mouths?

And am I then truly, truly exiled
while a river of burning water passes in the dark?
How many times you are the one hatred leaves nameless,
how, drowned in the shadows,
under a rain of pulverized dung
your statue devours the clover in my heart.

Hatred is a hammer beating on your clothing,
on your feverish face,
and the heart's days fall in your ears
like shadowy owls of eliminated blood
and the necklaces which were made of tears drop by drop
encircle your throat, branding your voice like ice.

This so you cannot
ever, ever talk, so that no single swallow
can ever wing out of the nest of your tongue
and so that nettles destroy your throat
and a harsh ship's wind inhabits you.

Where do you strip?
In a railway carriage for a randy Peruvian?
or by a harvester, among clods, in the violent
light of the wheat?
Or are you going now with certain evil-eyed solicitors
generously naked, running along night's shores?

Miras: no ves la luna ni el jacinto
ni la oscuridad goteada de humedades,
ni el tren de cieno, ni el marfil partido:
ves cinturas delgadas como oxígeno,
pechos que aguardan acumulando peso
e idéntica al zafiro de lunar avaricia
palpitas desde el dulce ombligo hasta las rosas.

Por qué sí? Por qué no? Los días descubiertos
aportan roja arena sin cesar destrozada
a las hélices puras que inauguran el día,
y pasa un mes con corteza de tortuga,
pasa un estéril día,
pasa un buey, un difunto,
una mujer llamada Rosalía,
y no queda en la boca sino un sabor de pelo
y de dorada lengua que con sed se alimenta.
Nada sino esa pulpa de los seres,
nada sino esa copa de raíces.

Yo persigo como en un túnel roto, en otro extremo
carne y besos que debo olvidar injustamente,
y en las aguas de espaldas cuando ya los espejos
avivan el abismo, cuando la fatiga, los sórdidos relojes
golpean a la puerta de hoteles suburbanos, y cae
la flor de papel pintado, y de terciopelo cagado por las ratas y la cama
cien veces ocupada por miserables parejas, cuando
todo me dice que un día ha terminado, tú y yo
hemos estado juntos derribando cuerpos,
construyendo una casa que no dura ni muere,
tú y yo hemos corrido juntos un mismo río
con encadenadas bocas llenas de sal y sangre,
tú y yo hemos hecho temblar otra vez las luces verdes
y hemos solicitado de nuevo las grandes cenizas.

Recuerdo sólo un día
que tal vez nunca me fue destinado,
era un día incesante,
sin orígenes. Jueves.
Yo era un hombre transportado al acaso
con una mujer hallada vagamente,
nos desnudamos

Look: you don't see the moon nor the jasmine,
nor the darkness misted over,
nor the train of silt, nor the cracked ivory:
but you see belts as thin as oxygen,
breasts patient with accumulated weight
and exactly as the sapphire of lunar avarice
you tremble from your lovely navel up to the roses.

Why? And why not? The naked days
bring this red sand ceaselessly decomposing
to the churning engines of the dawn
and a month goes by with the shell of a tortoise,
a barren day goes by,
an ox goes by, a funeral,
a woman whose name is Rosalía,
and nothing remains in the mouth save the taste of hair
and of golden tongue whose food is thirst.
Nothing if not this mush of beings,
nothing if not this grail of roots.

I persist as if in a ruined tunnel, at another limit,
flesh and kisses I must unjustly forget,
and in the water-weak shoulders, when the mirrors harrow
the depths, when weariness and sordid clocks
beat on the doors of suburban hotels,
the painted flower falls, the rat-shit-covered velvet,
the bed pathetic couples have rocked a hundred times –
and everything tells me a day has died, you and I
have been together overthrowing our bodies,
building a house that neither stands nor dies,
you and I have ridden together a single river
with locked mouths full of blood and salt,
you and I have set the green lights trembling again
and we have invoked once more the immeasurable ashes.

I remember no more than a day
which, who knows, was never destined for me,
an interminable day
which had never begun. Thursday.
I was a man put there by chance
meeting a woman by some vague arrangement.
We undressed

como para morir o nadar o envejecer
y nos metimos uno dentro del otro,
ella rodeándome como un agujero,
yo quebrantándola como quien
golpea una campana,
pues ella era el sonido que me hería
y la cúpula dura decidida a temblar.

Era una sorda ciencia con cabello y cavernas
y machacando puntas de médula y dulzura
he rodado a las grandes coronas genitales
entre piedras y asuntos sometidos.
Éste es un cuento de puertos adonde
llega uno, al azar, y sube a las colinas,
suceden tantas cosas.

Enemiga, enemiga,
es posible que el amor haya caído al polvo
y no haya sino carne y huesos velozmente adorados
mientras el fuego se consume
y los caballos vestidos de rojo galopan al infierno?

Yo quiero para mí la avena y el relámpago
a fondo de epidermis,
y el devorante pétalo desarrollado en furia,
y el corazón labial del cerezo de Junio,
y el reposo de lentas barrigas que arden sin dirección,
pero me falta un suelo de cal con lágrimas
y una ventana donde esperar espumas.

Así es la vida,
corre tú entre las hojas, un otoño
negro ha llegado,
corre vestida con una falda de hojas y un cinturón de metal amarillo,
mientras la neblina de la estación roe las piedras.
Corre con tus zapatos, con tus medias,
con el gris repartido, con el hueco del pie, y con esas manos que el tabaco salvaje
    adoraría,
golpea escaleras, derriba
el papel negro que protege las puertas,
y entra en medio del sol y la ira de un día de puñales
a echarte como paloma de luto y nieve sobre un cuerpo.

as if to die, or swim, or to grow old
and we put ourselves one into another,
she circling me like a pit,
I banging at her like a man
who would strike a bell
since she was the sound that wounded me
and the hard dome set on its own vibration.

It was some deaf science of hair and caverns
when, pounding piths and sweetnesses,
I circled the great wreaths of her sex
between stones and tributes.
This is a story of ports
where one arrives by chance and climbs the hills
and so many things come to pass.

Enemy, my enemy,
has love fallen to dust
and will nothing do save flesh and bone furiously adored
while the fire devours itself
and the red-harnessed horses rush into hell?

I want for myself oats and lightnings
in the folds of my skin
and the consuming petal unfurled in its fury
and the labial heart of the cherry tree in June,
and the repose of slow bellies aimlessly burning:
but I lack a chalk soil with tears
and a window to lean at waiting for waves.

That's life.
Run among the leaves. An autumn
black as soot has come down,
run in your skirt of leaves, with a yellow metal belt
while the hill-station mist corrodes the stones.
Run in your shoes, in your stockings,
in your grey divisions, with the hollow of your foot, and those hands
the wild tobacco would bless,
batter at stairways, tear down
the black paper blinds on these doors,
and come into the belt of the sun and the anger of a day of daggers
to throw yourself like a dove of mourning and snow upon a body.

Es una sola hora larga como una vena,
y entre el ácido y la paciencia del tiempo arrugado
transcurrimos,
apartando las sílabas del miedo y la ternura,
interminablemente exterminados.

There is one hour alone, long as an artery,
and between the acid and the patience of crumpled time
we voyage through
parting the syllables of fear and tenderness
interminably done away with, done to death.

[N.T.]

Explico algunas cosas

Preguntaréis: Y dónde están las lilas?
Y la metafísica cubierta de amapolas?
Y la lluvia que a menudo golpeaba
sus palabras llenándolas
de agujeros y pájaros?

Os voy a contar todo lo que me pasa.

Yo vivía en un barrio
de Madrid, con campanas,
con relojes, con árboles.

Desde allí se veía
el rostro seco de Castilla
como un océano de cuero.
                    Mi casa era llamada
la casa de las flores, porque por todas partes
estallaban geranios: era
una bella casa
con perros y chiquillos.
                    Raúl, te acuerdas?
Te acuerdas, Rafael?
                    Federico, te acuerdas
debajo de la tierra,
te acuerdas de mi casa con balcones en donde
la luz de junio ahogaba flores en tu boca?
                    Hermano, hermano!
Todo
eran grandes voces, sal de mercaderías,
aglomeraciones de pan palpitante,
mercados de mi barrio de Argüelles con su estatua
como un tintero pálido entre las merluzas:
el aceite llegaba a las cucharas,
un profundo latido
de pies y manos llenaba las calles,
metros, litros, esencia
aguda de la vida,
                    pescados hacinados,
contextura de techos con sol frío en el cual

I'm Explaining a Few Things

You are going to ask: and where are the lilacs?
and the poppy-petalled metaphysics?
and the rain repeatedly spattering
its words and drilling them full
of apertures and birds?

I'll tell you all the news.

I lived in a suburb,
a suburb of Madrid, with bells,
and clocks, and trees.

From there you could look out
over Castille's dry face:
a leather ocean.
⠀⠀⠀⠀⠀⠀⠀⠀⠀⠀My house was called
the house of flowers, because in every cranny
geraniums burst: it was
a good-looking house
with its dogs and children.
⠀⠀⠀⠀⠀⠀⠀⠀⠀⠀⠀⠀Remember, Raúl?
Eh, Rafael?
⠀⠀⠀⠀⠀⠀⠀⠀Federico, do you remember
from under the ground
my balconies on which
the light of June drowned flowers in your mouth?
⠀⠀⠀⠀⠀⠀⠀⠀⠀⠀⠀⠀⠀⠀⠀⠀⠀⠀Brother, my brother!
Everything
loud with big voices, the salt of merchandises,
pile-ups of palpitating bread,
the stalls of my suburb of Argüelles with its statue
like a drained inkwell in a swirl of hake:
oil flowed into spoons,
a deep baying
of feet and hands swelled in the streets,
metres, litres, the sharp
measure of life,
⠀⠀⠀⠀⠀⠀⠀⠀⠀⠀stacked-up fish,
the texture of roofs with a cold sun in which

la flecha se fatiga,
delirante marfil fino de las patatas,
tomates repetidos hasta el mar.

Y una mañana todo estaba ardiendo
y una mañana las hogueras
salían de la tierra
devorando seres,
y desde entonces fuego,
pólvora desde entonces,
y desde entonces sangre.
Bandidos con aviones y con moros,
bandidos con sortijas y duquesas,
bandidos con frailes negros bendiciendo
venían por el cielo a matar niños,
y por las calles la sangre de los niños
corría simplemente, como sangre de niños.

Chacales que el chacal rechazaría,
piedras que el cardo seco mordería escupiendo,
víboras que las víboras odiaran!

Frente a vosotros he visto la sangre
de España levantarse
para ahogaros en una sola ola
de orgullo y de cuchillos!

Generales
traidores:
mirad mi casa muerta,
mirad España rota:
pero de cada casa muerta sale metal ardiendo
en vez de flores,
pero de cada hueco de España
sale España,
pero de cada niño muerto sale un fusil con ojos,
pero de cada crimen nacen balas
que os hallarán un día el sitio
del corazón.

Preguntaréis por qué su poesía
no nos habla del sueño, de las hojas,

the weather vane falters,
the fine, frenzied ivory of potatoes,
wave on wave of tomatoes rolling down to the sea.

And one morning all that was burning,
one morning the bonfires
leapt out of the earth
devouring human beings –
and from then on fire,
gunpowder from then on,
and from then on blood.
Bandits with planes and Moors,
bandits with finger-rings and duchesses,
bandits with black friars spattering blessings
came through the sky to kill children
and the blood of children ran through the streets
without fuss, like children's blood.

Jackals that the jackals would despise,
stones that the dry thistle would bite on and spit out,
vipers that the vipers would abominate!

Face to face with you I have seen the blood
of Spain tower like a tide
to drown you in one wave
of pride and knives!

Treacherous
generals:
see my dead house,
look at broken Spain:
from every house burning metal flows
instead of flowers,
from every socket of Spain
Spain emerges
and from every dead child a rifle with eyes,
and from every crime bullets are born
which will one day find
the bull's eye of your hearts.

And you will ask: why doesn't his poetry
speak of dreams and leaves

de los grandes volcanes de su país natal?

Venid a ver la sangre por las calles.
venid a ver
la sangre por las calles,
venid a ver la sangre
por las calles!

and the great volcanoes of his native land?

Come and see the blood in the streets.
Come and see
the blood in the streets.
Come and see the blood
in the streets!

[N.T.]

Cómo era España

Era España tirante y seca, diurno
tambor de son opaco,
llanura y nido de águilas, silencio
de azotada intemperie.

Cómo, hasta el llanto, hasta el alma
amo tu duro suelo, tu pan pobre,
tu pueblo pobre, cómo hasta el hondo sitio
de mi ser hay la flor perdida de tus aldeas
arrugadas, inmóviles de tiempo,
y tus campiñas minerales
extendidas en luna y en edad
y devoradas por un dios vacío.

Todas tus estructuras, tu animal
aislamiento junto a tu inteligencia
rodeada por las piedras abstractas del silencio,
tu áspero vino, tu suave
vino, tus violentas
y delicadas viñas.

Piedra solar, pura entre las regiones
del mundo, España recorrida
por sangres y metales, azul y victoriosa,
proletaria de pétalos y balas, única
viva y soñolienta y sonora.

...

The Way Spain Was

Taut and dry Spain was,
a day's drum of dull sound,
a plain, an eagle's eyrie, a silence
below the lashing weather.

How unto crying out, unto the very soul
I love your barren soil and your rough bread,
your stricken people!
How in the depths of me
grows the lost flower of your villages,
timeless, impossible to budge,
your tracts of minerals
bulging like oldsters under the moon,
devoured by an imbecile god.

All your extensions, your bestial solitude,
joined with your sovereign intelligence,
haunted by the abstracted stones of silence,
your harsh wine and your sweet wine,
your violent and delicate vineyards.

Stone of the sun, pure among territories,
Spain veined with bloods and metals, blue and victorious,
proletariat of petals and bullets,
alone alive, somnolent, resounding.

· · ·

[N.T.]

from *Canto general* (1950)

Algunas bestias

Era el crepúsculo de la iguana.

Desde la arcoirisada crestería
su lengua como un dardo
se hundía en la verdura,
el hormiguero monacal pisaba
con melodioso pie la selva,
el guanaco fino como el oxígeno
en las anchas alturas pardas
iba calzando botas de oro,
mientras la llama abría cándidos
ojos en la delicadeza
del mundo lleno de rocío.
Los monos trenzaban un hilo
interminablemente erótico
en las riberas de la aurora,
derribando muros de polen
y espantando el vuelo violeta
de las mariposas de Muzo.
Era la noche pura y pululante
de hocicos saliendo del légamo,
y de las ciénagas soñolientas
un ruido opaco de armaduras
volvía al origen terrestre.

El jaguar tocaba las hojas
con su ausencia fosforescente,
el puma corre en el ramaje
como el fuego devorador
mientras arden en él los ojos
alcohólicos de la selva.
Los tejones rascan los pies
del río, husmean el nido
cuya delicia palpitante
atacarán con dientes rojos.

Y en el fondo del agua magna,
como el círculo de la tierra,

Some Beasts

It was early twilight of the iguana.

From his rainbow-crested ridging
his tongue sank like a dart
into the mulch,
the monastic ant-heap was melodiously
teeming in the undergrowth,
the guanaco, rarefied as oxygen
up among the cloud-plains,
wore gold-flecked boots,
while the llama opened candid
wide eyes in the delicacy
of a world filled with dew.
The monkeys wove a thread
interminably erotic
along the banks of dawn,
demolishing walls of pollen
and flushing the violet flight
of the butterflies from Buga.
It was night of the alligators,
pure and pullulating night
of snouts above the ooze
and from over the sleep-drenched bogs
a dull sound of armour
fell back upon the original earth.

The jaguar touches the leaves
with his phosphorescent absence,
the puma runs on the foliage
like all-consuming flame
and in him burn
the alcoholic eyes of the jungle.
The badgers scratch the river's
feet, scenting out the nest
whose throbbing delight
they'll assail red-toothed.

And in the deeps of great water
the giant anaconda lies

está la gigante anaconda
cubierta de barros rituales,
devoradora y religiosa.

like the circle of the earth,
covered in ritual mud,
devouring and religious

[A.K.]

XI

A través del confuso esplendor,
a través de la noche de piedra, déjame hundir la mano
y deja que en mí palpite, como un ave mil años prisionera,
el viejo corazón del olvidado!
Déjame olvidar hoy esta dicha, que es más ancha que el mar,
porque el hombre es más ancho que el mar y que sus islas,
y hay que caer en él como en un pozo para salir del fondo
con un ramo de agua secreta y de verdades sumergidas.
Déjame olvidar, ancha piedra, la proporción poderosa,
la trascendente medida, las piedras del panal,
y de la escuadra déjame hoy resbalar
la mano sobre la hipotenusa de áspera sangre y cilicio.
Cuando, como una herradura de élitros rojos, el cóndor furibundo
me golpea las sienes en el orden del vuelo
y el huracán de plumas carniceras barre el polvo sombrío
de las escalinatas diagonales, no veo a la bestia veloz,
no veo el ciego ciclo de sus garras,
veo el antiguo ser, servidor, el dormido
en los campos, veo un cuerpo, mil cuerpos, un hombre, mil mujeres,
bajo la racha negra, negros de lluvia y noche,
con la piedra pesada de la estatua:
Juan Cortapiedras, hijo de Wiracocha,
Juan Comefrío, hijo de estrella verde,
Juan Piesdescalzos, nieto de la turquesa,
sube a nacer conmigo, hermano.

from *The Heights of Macchu Picchu*

XI

Through a confusion of splendour,
through a night made stone let me plunge my hand
and move to beat in me a bird held for a thousand years,
the old and unremembered human heart!
Today let me forget this happiness, wider than all the sea,
because man is wider than all the sea and her necklace of islands
and we must fall into him as down a well to clamber back with
branches of secret water, recondite truths.
Allow me to forget, circumference of stone, the powerful proportions,
the transcendental span, the honeycomb's foundations,
and from the set-square allow my hand to slide
down a hypotenuse of hairshirt and salt blood.
When, like a horseshore of rusting wing-cases, the furious condor
batters my temples in the order of flight
and his tornado of carnivorous feathers sweeps the dark dust
down slanting stairways, I do not see the rush of the bird,
nor the blind sickle of his talons –
I see the ancient being, the slave, the sleeping one,
blanket his fields – a body, a thousand bodies, a man, a thousand
women swept by the sable whirlwind, charred with rain and night,
stoned with a leaden weight of statuary:
Juan Splitstones, son of Wiracocha,
Juan Coldbelly, heir of the green star,
Juan Barefoot, grandson to the turquoise,
rising to birth with me, as my own brother.

[N.T.]

Vienen por las islas (1493)

Los carniceros desolaron las islas.
Guanahaní fue la primera
en esta historia de martirios.
Los hijos de la arcilla vieron rota
su sonrisa, golpeada
su frágil estatura de venados,
y aun en la muerte no entendían.
Fueron amarrados y heridos,
fueron quemados y abrasados,
fueron mordidos y enterrados.
Y cuando el tiempo dio su vuelta de vals
bailando en las palmeras,
el salón verde estaba vacío.

Sólo quedaban huesos
rígidamente colocados
en forma de cruz, para mayor
gloria de Dios y de los hombres.

De las gredas mayorales
y el ramaje de Sotavento
hasta las agrupadas coralinas
fue cortando el cuchillo de Narváez.
Aquí la cruz, aquí el rosario,
aquí la Virgen del Garrote.
La alhaja de Colón, Cuba fosfórica,
recibió el estandarte y las rodillas
en su arena mojada.

They Come for the Islands (1493)

The butchers laid waste the islands.
Guanahaní was the first
in that history of torments.
The children of clay saw their
smiles smashed, battered
their stance slight as deers',
all the way to death they did not understand.
They were trussed up and tortured,
they were lit and burned,
they were gnawed and buried.
And when time danced around again
waltzing among the palms
the green hall was empty.

    Nothing was left but bones
    rigidly fastened
    in the form of a cross, to the greater
    glory of God and of men.

    From the chief clay-pits
    and green boughs of Sotavento
    to the coral cays
    the knife of Narváez went carving.
    Here the cross, here the rosary,
    here the Virgin of the Stake.
    Glowing Cuba, Columbus's jewel,
    received the standard and the knees
    in its wet sand.

[W.S.M.]

Descubridores de Chile

Del Norte trajo Almagro su arrugada centella.
Y sobre el territorio, entre explosión y ocaso,
se inclinó día y noche como sobre una carta.
Sombra de espinas, sombra de cardo y cera,
el español reunido con su seca figura,
mirando las sombrías estrategias del suelo.
Noche, nieve y arena hacen la forma
de mi delgada patria,
todo el silencio está en su larga línea,
toda la espuma sale de su barba marina,
todo el carbón la llena de misteriosos besos.
Como una brasa el oro arde en sus dedos
y la plata ilumina como una luna verde
su endurecida forma de tétrico planeta.
El español sentado junto a la rosa un día,
junto al aceite, junto al vino, junto al antiguo cielo
no imaginó este punto de colérica piedra
nacer bajo el estiércol del águila marina.

Discoverers of Chile

From the north Almagro brought his crushed ember.
And over the territory, between explosion and sunset,
he bent, day and night, as over a chart.
Shadow of thorns, shadow of thistle and wax,
the Spaniard meeting with his dry figure,
watching the sombre strategies of the terrain.
Night, snow, and sand make up the form
of my thin country,
all silence lies in its long line,
all foam flows from its marine beard,
all coal covers it with mysterious kisses.
Gold burns in its fingers like an ember
and silver illuminates like a green moon
its thickened shadow of a sullen planet.
The Spaniard seated by the rose one day,
by the olive oil, by the wine, by the antique sky,
did not imagine this point of choleric stone
being born from under the dung of the sea eagle.

[A.K.]

El corazón Magallánico (1519)

De dónde soy, me pregunto a veces, de dónde diablos
vengo, qué día es hoy, qué pasa,
ronco, en medio del sueño, del árbol, de la noche,
y una ola se levanta como un párpado, un día
nace de ella, un relámpago con hocico de tigre.

DESPIERTO
DE PRONTO
EN LA
NOCHE
PENSANDO
EN EL
EXTREMO
SUR

Viene el día y me dice: 'Oyes
el agua lenta, el agua,
el agua,
sobre la Patagonia?'
Y yo contesto: 'Sí, señor, escucho'.
Viene el día y me dice: 'Una oveja salvaje
lejos, en la región, lame el color helado
de una piedra. No escuchas el balido, no reconoces
el vendaval azul en cuyas manos
la luna es una copa, no ves la tropa, el dedo
rencoroso del viento
tocar la ola y la vida con su anillo vacío?'

RECUERDO
LA SOLEDAD
DEL
ESTRECHO

La larga noche, el pino, vienen adonde voy.
Y se trastorna el ácido sordo, la fatiga,
la tapa del tonel, cuanto tengo en la vida.
Una gota de nieve llora y llora en mi puerta
mostrando su vestido claro y desvencijado
de pequeño cometa que me busca y solloza.
Nadie mira la ráfaga, la extensión, el aullido
del aire en las praderas.
Me acerco y digo: vamos. Toco el Sur, desemboco
en la arena, veo la planta seca y negra, todo raíz y roca,
las islas arañadas por el agua y el cielo,
el Río del Hambre, el Corazón de Ceniza,
el Patio del Mar Lúgubre, y donde silba
la solitaria serpiente, donde cava
el último zorro herido y esconde su tesoro sangriento
encuentro la tempestad y su voz de ruptura,
su voz de viejo libro, su boca de cien labios,
algo me dice, algo que el aire devora cada día.

The Magellan Heart (1519)

Where am I from, where in the devil do I come from,
I sometimes ask myself, what day is it today, what's going on,
I snore, in the middle of a dream, a tree, a night,
and a wave is raised like an eyelid, a day
is born from the wave, a lightning-bolt with a tiger's snout.

I SUDDENLY
AWAKE IN
THE NIGHT
THINKING
OF THE FAR
SOUTH

The day comes and says: 'Do you hear
the slow water, the water,
the water
over Patagonia?'
And I answer: 'Yes, sir, I'm listening.'
The day comes and says: 'A wild sheep
far away, in this region, licks the frozen colour
of a stone. Aren't you listening to the bleating, don't you
   recognize
the blue squall in whose hands
the moon is a goblet, don't you see the drove, the rancorous
finger of the wind
touching wave and life with its empty ring?'

I RECALL
THE
SOLITUDE
OF THE
STRAIT

The long night, the pine, come where I go.
And the stifled acid is overturned, and fatigue,
the barrel-top, whatever I have in life.
A snowdrop weeps and weeps at my door
exhibiting the sheer loose-limbed dress
of a tiny comet seeking me out and sobbing.
No one observes the gust of wind, its expanse,
its howling through the prairies.
I approach and say: Let's go. I touch the South, flow
into the sand, see the dry blackened plant, all root and rock,
the islands scraped by water and sky,
Hunger River, Heart of Ashes,
Patio of the Dismal Sea, and, where
the solitary serpent hisses, where
the last wounded fox digs to hide its bloody treasures,
I meet the storm and its voice of rupture,
its voice from an old book, its hundred-lipped mouth,
and it tells me something, something the wind devours every
   day.

LOS
DESCUBRI-
DORES
APARECEN
Y DE ELLOS
NO QUEDA
NADA
Recuerda el agua cuanto le sucedió al navío.
La dura tierra extraña guarda sus calaveras
que suenan en el pánico austral como cornetas
y ojos de hombre y de buey, dan al día su hueco,
su anillo, su sonido de implacable estelaje.
El viejo cielo busca la vela,
                     nadie
ya sobrevive: el buque destruido
vive con la ceniza del marinero amargo,
y de los puestos de oro, de las casas de cuero
del trigo pestilente, y de
la llama fría de las navegaciones
(cuánto golpe en la noche [roca y bajel] al fondo)
sólo queda el dominio quemado y sin cadáveres,
la incesante intemperie apenas rota
por un negro fragmento
de fuego fallecido.

Esfera que destroza lentamente la noche, el agua, el hielo,
extensión combatida por el tiempo y el término,
con su marca violeta, con el final azul
del arco iris salvaje
se sumergen los pies de mi patria en tu sombra
y aúlla y agoniza la rosa triturada.

Por el canal navega nuevamente
el cereal helado, la barba del combate,
el Otoño glacial, el transitorio herido.
Con él, con el antiguo, con el muerto,
con el destituído por el agua rabiosa,
con él, en su tormenta, con su frente.
Aún lo sigue el albatros y la soga de cuero
comida, con los ojos fuera de la mirada,
y el ratón devorado ciegamente mirando
entre los palos rotos el esplendor iracundo,
mientras en el vacío la sortija y el hueso
caen, resbalan sobre la vaca marina.

Cuál es el dios que pasa? Mirad su barba llena de gusanos
y sus calzones en que la espesa atmósfera
se pega y muerde como un perro náufrago:
y tiene peso de ancla maldita su estatura,

THE DIS-
COVERERS
APPEAR
AND OF
THEM
NOTHING
REMAINS

The water remembers what happened to the ship.
The hard foreign earth shelters their skulls
which resound in the southern panic like bugles,
and the eyes of man and ox lend the day their hollow,
their ring, their sound of implacable wake.
The old sky looks for the sail,
                              nobody
now survives: the wrecked ship
lives with the acrid sailor's ashes,
and of the gold-stalls, the leather houses
of pestilent wheat, of
the cold flame of voyages
(what blows strike in the night [rock on boat] at the bottom!)
all that remains is the burnt-out, corpseless domain,
the ceaseless rough weather scarce broken
by a black fragment
of dead fire.

DESO-
LATION
REIGNS
ALONE

Sphere slowly shattered by the night, the water, the ice,
space overcome by time and termination:
violet-veined with the ultimate blue
of a wild rainbow
my country's feet lie submerged in your shadow
and the battered rose keens in its agony.

I RECALL
THE
ANCIENT
DISCOVERER

Once again along the channel sails
the frozen wheat, the corn-bread of combat,
the Glacial Fall, the transitory casualty.
They sail with him, the Old Man, the dead man
exiled by the furious water,
with him, in turmoil, with his front.
Still the albatross follows and the frayed leather
rope, his eyes wandered out of his head,
the rat blindly swallowed, staring
through the rent masts at the splendour of wrath,
while through the void the ring and bone
fall, sliding off a manatee.

MAGELLAN

What god is that going by? Look at his maggoty beard
and his trousers stuck with heavy weather
bitten by thick air like a shipwrecked dog:
his height weighs like a foundered anchor,

y silba el piélago y el aquilón acude
hasta sus pies mojados.

Caracol de la oscura

sombra del tiempo,

espuela

carcomida, viejo señor de luto litoral, aguilero
sin estirpe, manchado manantial, el estiércol
del Estrecho te manda,
y no tiene de cruz tu pecho sino un grito
del mar, un grito blanco, de luz marina,
y de la tenaza, de tumbo en tumbo, de aguijón demolido.

LLEGA AL
PACÍFICO

Porque el siniestro día del mar termina un día,
y la mano nocturna corta uno a uno sus dedos
hasta no ser, hasta que el hombre nace
y el capitán descubre dentro de sí el acero
y la América sube su burbuja
y la costa levanta su pálido arrecife
sucio de aurora, turbio de nacimiento
hasta que de la nave sale un grito y se ahoga
y otro grito y el alba que nace de la espuma.

TODOS HAN
MUERTO

Hermanos de agua y piojo, de planeta carnívoro:
visteis, al fin, el árbol del mástil agachado
por la tormenta? Visteis la piedra machacada
bajo la loca nieve brusca de la ráfaga?
Al fin, ya tenéis vuestro paraíso perdido,
al fin, tenéis vuestra guarnición maldiciente,
al fin, vuestros fantasmas atravesados del aire
besan sobre la arena la huella de la foca.
Al fin, a vuestros dedos sin sortija
llega el pequeño sol del páramo, el día muerto,
temblando, en su hospital de olas y piedras.

and the sea hisses, the north wind flies
up to his wet feet.
                              Caracol from out of the dark
shadow of time,
                              spur
gnawed away, old lord of littoral keening, eagle-aerie
without pedigree, tainted well, the Straits' guano
directs you,
and your breast bears no cross beyond a shout
from the sea, a white shout of marine light
and claw, from fall to fall, of washed-out goad.

HE REACHES   Since one day the sinister sea's day ends
THE   and the nocturnal hand cuts off its fingers one by one
PACIFIC   till it is not, till the man is born
and the Captain discovers steel within himself
and America raises its bubble
and the coast proffers its pale reef
dank with dawn, turbid with birth
till a shout comes from the ship and is drowned
and then another shout and dawn is born from the foam.

THEY ALL   Brothers of the water and the lice, of the carnivorous planet:
HAVE DIED   did you see at the last the mast-tree bend
to the storm? Did you see the stone crushed
beneath the mad sudden snow of the squall?
At the last, your paradise is lost,
at the last, your garrison accursed,
at the last, your phantoms transfixed by air
kissing the tread of the seal in the sand.
At the last, the small sun of the paramo, the dead day,
trembling, in its hospital of waves and stones,
reaches your ringless fingers.

[A.K.]

A pesar de la ira

Roídos yelmos, herraduras muertas!

Pero a través del fuego y la herradura
como de un manantial iluminado
por la sangre sombría,
con el metal hundido en el tormento
se derramó una luz sobre la tierra:
número, nombre, línea y estructura.

Páginas de agua, claro poderío
de idiomas rumorosos, dulces gotas
elaboradas como los racimos,
sílabas de platino en la ternura
de unos aljofarados pechos puros,
y una clásica boca de diamantes
dio su fulgor nevado al territorio.

Allá lejos la estatua deponía
su mármol muerto,
                            y en la primavera
del mundo, amaneció la maquinaria.

La técnica elevaba su dominio
y el tiempo fue velocidad y ráfaga
en la bandera de los mercaderes.

Luna de geografía
que descubrió la planta y el planeta
extendiendo geométrica hermosura
en su desarrollado movimiento.
Asia entregó su virginal aroma.
La inteligenica con un hilo helado
fue detrás de la sangre hilando el día.
El papel repartió la miel desnuda
guardada en las tinieblas.

Un vuelo
de palomar salió de la pintura
con arrebol y azul ultramarino.

In Spite of Wrath

Corroded helmets, dead horseshoes!

But through the fire and the horseshoe
as from a wellspring illuminated
by murky blood,
along with the metal thrust home in the holocaust
a light fell over the earth:
number, name, line and structure.

Pages of water, clear power
of murmuring tongues, sweet drops
worked like clusters,
platinum syllables in the tenderness
of dew-streaked breasts,
and a classic diamond mouth
gave its snowy brillance to the land

In the distance the statue asserted
its dead marble,
                    and in the spring
of the world, machinery dawned.

Technique erected its dominion
and time became speed and a flash
on the banner of the merchants.

Moon of geography
that discovered plant and planet
extending geometric beauty
in its unfolding movement.
Asia handed up its virginal scent.
Intelligence, with a frozen thread,
followed behind blood, spinning out the day.
The paper called for the distribution of the naked honey
kept in the darkness.

A pigeon-house
flight was flushed from the painting
in sunset-cloud-red and ultramarine blue.

Y las lenguas del hombre se juntaron
en la primera ira, antes del canto.

Así, con el sangriento
titán de piedra,
halcón encarnizado,
no sólo llegó sangre sino trigo.

La luz vino a pesar de los puñales.

And the tongues of men were joined
in the first wrath, before song.

Thus, with the sanguinary
titan of stone,
infuriated falcon,
came not only blood but wheat.

Light came despite the daggers.

[A.K.]

Educación del cacique

Lautaro era una flecha delgada.
Elástico y azul fue nuestro padre.
Fue su primera edad sólo silencio.
Su adolescencia fue dominio.
Su juventud fue un viento dirigido.
Se preparó como una larga lanza.
Acostumbró los pies en las cascadas.
Educó la cabeza en las espinas.
Ejecutó las pruebas del guanaco.
Vivió en las madrigueras de la nieve.
Acechó la comida de las águilas.
Arañó los secretos del peñasco.
Entretuvo los pétalos del fuego.
Se amamantó de primavera fría.
Se quemó en las gargantas infernales.
Fue cazador entre las aves crueles.
Se tiñeron sus mantos de victorias.
Leyó las agresiones de la noche.
Sostuvo los derrumbes del azufre.

Se hizo velocidad, luz repentina.

Tomó las lentitudes del Otoño.
Trabajó en las guaridas invisibles.
Durmió en las sábanas del ventisquero.
Igualó la conducta de las flechas.
Bebió la sangre agreste en los caminos.
Arrebató el tesoro de las olas.
Se hizo amenaza como un dios sombrío.
Comió en cada cocina de su pueblo.
Aprendió el alfabeto del relámpago.
Olfateó las cenizas esparcidas.
Envolvió el corazón con pieles negras.

Descifró el espiral hilo del humo.
Se construyó de fibras taciturnas.
Se aceitó como el alma de la oliva.
Se hizo cristal de transparencia dura.

Education of the Chieftain

Lautaro*was a slender arrow.
Supple and blue was our father.
His first years were all silence.
His adolescence authority.
His youth an aimed wind.
He trained himself like a long lance.
He habituated his feet in cascades.
He schooled his head among thorns.
He executed the essays of the guanaco.
He lived in the burrows of the snow.
He ambushed the prey of eagles.
He scratched the secrets from crags.
He allayed the petals of fire.
He suckled cold springtime.
He burned in infernal gorges.
He was a hunter among cruel birds.
His mantle was stained with victories.
He perused the night's aggressions.
He bore the sulphur landslides.

He made himself velocity, sudden light.

He took on the lassitude of Autumn.
He worked in the invisible haunts.
He slept under the sheets of snowdrifts.
He equalled the conduct of arrows.
He drank wild blood on the roads.
He wrested treasure from the waves.
He made himself menace, like a sombre god.
He ate from each fire of his people.
He learned the alphabet of the lightning.
He scented the scattered ash.
He wrapped his heart in black skins.

He deciphered the spiral thread of smoke.
He made himself out of taciturn fibres.
He oiled himself like the soul of the olive.
He became glass of transparent hardness.

   *An Araucanian chieftain (translator's note).

Estudió para viento huracanado.
Se combatió hasta apagar la sangre.

Sólo entonces fue digno de su pueblo.

He studied to be a hurricane wind.
He fought himself until his blood was extinguished.

Only then was he worthy of his people.

[A.K.]

Los peces y el ahogado

De pronto vi pobladas las regiones
de intensidad, de formas aceradas,
bocas como una línea que cortaba,
relámpagos de plata sumergida,
peces de luto, peces ojivales,
peces de firmamento tachonado,
peces cuyos lunares resplandecen,
peces que cruzan como escalofríos,
blanca velocidad, ciencias delgadas
de la circulación, bocas ovales
de la carnicería y el aumento.

Hermosa fue la mano o la cintura
que rodeada de luna fugitiva
vio trepidar la población pesquera,
húmedo río elástico de vidas,
crecimiento de estrella en las escamas,
ópalo seminal diseminado
en la sábana oscura del océano.

Vio arder las piedras de plata que mordían,
estandartes de trémulo tesoro,
y sometió su sangre descendiendo
a la profundidad devoradora,
suspendido por bocas que recorren
su torso con sortijas sanguinarias
hasta que desgreñado y dividido
como espiga sangrienta, es un escudo
de la marea, un traje que trituran
las amatistas, una herencia herida
bajo el mar, en el árbol numeroso.

The Fish and the Drowned Man

Suddenly I saw the environs intensely
populated, with steely forms,
mouths like cutting edges,
lightning-bolts of submerged silver,
fish in mourning, ogive-fish,
fish of a gilt-nailed firmament,
fish with flashing polka dots,
fish criss-crossing like chills,
a white velocity, a thin science
of circulation, the oval mouths
of havoc and growth.

The hand or waist was handsome
which, surrounded by a fugitive moon,
saw the fishery denizens teeming,
a humid river elastic with lives,
an increment of stars along the scales,
seminal opal disseminated
on the murky ocean's bedsheet.

He saw the silver stones that bit him burn,
banners of a tremulous treasure,
and he submitted his blood as he descended
to the devouring depths,
suspended from mouths that circle
his torso with sanguinary rings
until, dishevelled and divided,
like an oozing stem, he is the escutcheon
of the tide, a suit pounded
by amethysts, a wounded inheritance
under the sea, on the numerous tree.

[A.K.]

Rapa Nui

Tepito-Te-Henúa, ombligo del mar grande,
taller del mar, extinguida diadema.
De tu lava escorial subió la frente
del hombre más arriba del Océano,
los ojos agrietados de la piedra
midieron el ciclónico universo,
y fue central la mano que elevaba
la pura magnitud de tus estatuas.

Tu roca religiosa fue cortada
hacia todas las líneas del Océano
y los rostros del hombre aparecieron
surgiendo de la entraña de las islas,
naciendo de los cráteres vacíos
con los pies enredados al silencio.

Fueron los centinelas y cerraron
el ciclo de las aguas que llegaban
desde todos los húmedos dominios,
y el mar frente a las máscaras detuvo
sus tempestuosos árboles azules.
Nadie sino los rostros habitaron
el círculo del reino. Era callado
como la entrada de un planeta, el hilo
que envolvía la boca de la isla.

Así, en la luz del ábside marino
la fábula de piedra condecora
la inmensidad con sus medallas muertas,
y los pequeños reyes que levantan
toda esta solitaria monarquía
para la eternidad de las espumas,
vuelven al mar en la noche invisible,
vuelven a sus sarcófagos de sal.

Sólo el pez luna que murió en la arena.

Sólo el tiempo que muerde los moais.

Rapa Nui*

Tepito-Te-Henúa, omphalos of the Ocean,
workshop of the sea, extinguished diadem.
From your slag lava rose the forehead
of man above the Ocean;
the slit eyes of the stone
measured the cyclonic universe,
and the hand that raised
the pure magnitude of your statues was centric.

Your religious rock was cut
towards all the lines of Ocean
and the faces of man appeared
issuing from the matrix of islands,
born from the empty craters
their feet entwined in silence.

They were the sentinels and they closed
the cycle of the waters that surged
from all the wet domains,
and the sea, facing the masks, detained
their tempestuous blue trees.
No one but the face inhabited
the orbit of the kingdom. It was as silent
as the entrance to a planet, the thread
which enveloped the mouth of the island.

Thus, in the light of the marine apse
the stone fable decorates
the immensity with its defunct medals,
and the small kings who mount
this whole solitary monarchy
for the eternity of sea-foam
return to the sea in the invisible night,
return to their sarcophagi of salt.

Only, the moon fish which died in the sand.

Only, time which gnaws away at the moa birds.
  * Easter Island (translator's note).

Sólo la eternidad en las arenas
conocen las palabras:
la luz sellada, el laberinto muerto,
las llaves de la copa sumergida.

Only, the eternity in the sands
knowing the words:
the sealed light, the dead labyrinth,
the keys to the submerged bowl.

[A.K.]

Los navíos

Los barcos de la seda sobre la luz llevados,
erigidos en la violeta matutina,
cruzando el sol marítimo con rojos pabellones
deshilachados como estambres andrajosos,
el olor caluroso de las cajas doradas
que la canela hizo sonar como violines,
y la codicia fría que susurró en los puertos
en una tempestad de manos restregadas,
las bienvenidas suavidades verdes
de los jades, y el pálido cereal de la seda,
todo paseó en el mar como un viaje del viento,
como un baile de anémonas que desaparecieron.

Vinieron las delgadas velocidades, finas
herramientas del mar, peces de trapo,
dorados por el trigo, destinados
por sus mercaderías cenicientas,
por piedras desbordantes que brillaron
como el fuego cayendo entre sus velas,
o repletos de flores sulfurosas
recogidas en páramos salinos.
Otros cargaron razas, dispusieron
en la humedad de abajo, encadenados,
ojos cautivos que agrietaron con lágrimas
la pesada madera del navío.

Pies recién separados del marfil, amarguras
amontonadas como frutos malheridos,
dolores desollados como ciervos: cabezas
que desde los diamantes del verano cayeron
a la profundidad del estiércol infame.
Barcos llenos de trigo que temblaron
sobre las olas como en las llanuras
el viento cereal de las espigas:
naves de las ballenas, erizadas
de corazones duros como harpones,
lentas de cacería, desplazando
hacia Valparaíso sus bodegas,
velas grasientas que se sacudieron

The Ships

The silk ships over the light waves lofting,
erect in the violet dawn,
crossing the maritime sun with red ensigns
ravelled like ragged yarns,
with ardent odour of gilt boxes
which cinnamon had made resound like violins,
and the cold greed which whispered in the ports
in a tempest of scrubbed hands,
the green welcome suavities
of jades, and the pallid cereal of silk,
everything strolled on the sea like a voyage of wind,
like a dance of disappearing anemones.

The delicate velocities came on, fine-honed
sea-tools, sailing-fish,
golden in their wheat, destined
by their cinderella cargoes,
by the super-ballast stones which shone
like fire falling between their sails,
or brimful of sulphurous flowers
gathered in briny highlands.
Other ships bore races, disposed
about the humid bottoms, chained,
captive eyes that cracked the heavy wood
of ship's planks with tears:

　　their feet but barely out from ivory, mounds
　　of bitter fruit, like damaged produce,
　　dolours like excoriated deer: heads
　　fallen from the diamonds of summer
　　into the sloughs of despicable manure.
　　Ships filled with wheat trembling
　　on the waves as on the plains
　　the cereal wind in the tassels.
　　Whalers covered all over and barbed
　　with hearts hard as harpoons:
　　slow in the chase, displacing
　　their holds towards Valparaiso:
　　greasy sails flapping in the wind

heridas por el hielo y el aceite
hasta colmar las copas de la nave
con la cosecha blanda de la bestia.
Barcas desmanteladas que cruzaron
de tumbo en tumbo en el furor marino
con el hombre agarrado a sus recuerdos
y a los andrajos últimos del buque,
antes que, como manos cercenadas,
los fragmentos del mar los condujeran
a las delgadas bocas que poblaron
el espumoso mar en su agonía.
Naves de los nitratos, aguzadas
y alegres, como indómitos delfines
hacia las siete espumas deslizadas
por el viento en sus sábanas gloriosas,
finas como los dedos y las uñas,
veloces como plumas y corceles,
navegadoras de la mar morena
que pica los metales de mi patria.

lacerated by ice and oil
until the topmast bower heaped
with the bland harvest of the beast.
Unmasted ships criss-crossing
as they careen over and again in the sea-fury,
the men grappled to their memories
and the final tatters of the ship
before the fragments of the sea,
like severed hands, led them
to the thin mouths inhabiting
the foamy sea in its death agony.
Nitrate ships, whetted
and gay, like indominable dolphins,
bound for the seven sprays made lubricous
by the wind in its glorious sheets,
as fine as fingers and fingernails,
swift as feathers and neighing chargers,
navigators of the darksome sea
that pries at the metals of my land.

[A.K.]

A una estatua de proa (Elegía)

En las arenas de Magallanes te recogimos cansada
navegante, inmóvil
bajo la tempestad que tantas veces tu pecho dulce y doble
desafió dividiendo en sus pezones.

Te levantamos otra vez sobre los mares del Sur, pero ahora
fuiste la pasajera de lo obscuro, de los rincones, igual
al trigo y al metal que custodiaste
en alta mar, envuelta por la noche marina.

    Hoy eres mía, diosa que el albatros gigante
rozó con su estatura extendida en el vuelo,
como un manto de música dirigida en la lluvia
por tus ciegos y errantes párpados de madera.

    Rosa del mar, abeja más pura que los sueños,
almendrada mujer que desde las raíces
de una encina poblada por los cantos
te hiciste forma, fuerza de follaje con nidos,
boca de tempestades, dulzura delicada
que iría conquistando la luz con sus caderas.

    Cuando ángeles y reinas que nacieron contigo
se llenaron de musgo, durmieron destinadas
a la inmovilidad con un honor de muertos,
tú subiste a la proa delgada del navío
y ángel y reina y ola, temblor del mundo fuiste.
El estremecimiento de los hombres subía
hasta tu noble túnica con pechos de manzana,
mientras tus labios eran oh dulce! humedecidos
por otros besos dignos de tu boca salvaje.

    Bajo la noche extraña tu cintura dejaba
caer el peso puro de la nave en las olas
cortando en la sombría magnitud un camino
de fuego derribado, de miel fosforescente.
El viento abrió en tus rizos su caja tempestuosa,
el desencadenado metal de su gemido,

To a Ship's Figurehead (Elegy)

On the sands of Magellan we found you weary
navigator, unmoving
in the tempest which so often your sweet and twofold
breast defied cleaving it with your nipples.

We raised you once more above the Southern seas, but now
you were the passenger of the obscure, of the corners, equal
to the wheat and metal you kept
on the high seas, wrapped in the maritime night.

   Today you're mine, goddess whom the giant albatross
   grazed with its stature extended in flight,
   like a mantle of music conducted in the rain
   by your blind and errant wooden eyelids.

   Rose of the sea, bee purer than dreams,
   almond woman who from the roots
   of an oak peopled with song
   made yourself form, force of foliage with nests,
   mouth of storms, delicate sweetness
   who would go out conquering light with her thighs.

   When the angels and queens who were born with you
   covered themselves with moss, they slept destined
   to immobility with an honour guard of the dead,
   you climbed the thin prow of the ship,
   and, angel and queen and wave, you were the tremor of the world.
   The shuddering of men rose
   up to your noble tunic with its apple breasts
   while your lips – O sweet! – were wetted
   by other kisses worth your wild mouth.

   Under the strange night your waist let
   fall the pure weight of the ship in the waves
   cutting in the sombre magnitude a way
   of overthrown fire, of phosphorescent honey.
   The wind opened in your curls its tempestuous box
   the unchained metal of its howl,

y en la aurora la luz te recibió temblando
en los puertos, besando tu diadema mojada.

A veces detuviste sobre el mar tu camino
y el barco tembloroso bajó por su costado,
como una gruesa fruta que se desprende y cae,
un marinero muerto que acogieron la espuma
y el movimiento puro del tiempo y del navío.
Y sólo tú entre todos los rostros abrumados
por la amenaza, hundidos en un dolor estéril,
recibiste la sal salpicada en tu máscara,
y tus ojos guardaron las lágrimas saladas.
Más de una pobre vida resbaló por tus brazos
hacia la eternidad de las aguas mortuorias,
y el roce que te dieron los muertos y los vivos
gastó tu corazón de madera marina.

Hoy hemos recogido de la arena tu forma.
Al final, a mis ojos estabas destinada.
Duermes tal vez, dormida, tal vez has muerto, muerta:
tu movimiento, al fin, ha olvidado el susurro
y el esplendor errante cerró su travesía.
Iras del mar, golpes del cielo han coronado
tu altanera cabeza con grietas y rupturas,
y tu rostro como una caracola reposa
con heridas que marcan tu frente balanceada.

Para mí tu belleza guarda todo el perfume,
todo el ácido errante, toda su noche oscura.
Y en tu empinado pecho de lámpara o de diosa,
torre turgente, inmóvil amor, vive la vida.
Tú navegas conmigo, recogida, hasta el día
en que dejen caer lo que soy en la espuma.

and in the dawn the light received you trembling
in the ports, kissing your wet diadem.

Sometimes you held back your ship's way at sea
and the tremulous vessel fell away to port
like a thick fruit which breaks and falls off
a dead seaman whom the spray
and the pure movement of time and the ship pick up.
And only you among all the faces submerged
by the threat, sunken in a sterile sorrow,
received the splashed brine on your mask,
and your eyes retained the salty tears.
More than one poor life slithered from your arms
towards the eternity of mortuary waters,
and the rubbing contact of the dead and the quick
expended your marine-wood heart.

Today we picked up your form from the sand.
In the end, you were destined for my eyes.
Doubtless, sleeper, you're sleeping; perhaps, dead one, you're dead;
at long last your coming-and-going has forgotten
sea's sound, errant splendour has ceased its wandering.
You'll leave the sea, blows from heaven have crowned
your haughty head with fissures and cracks,
and your face like a conch shell reposes
with the wounds which mark your immutable forehead.

For me your beauty preserves all the perfume,
all the errant acid, all its dark night.
And in your high breasts of goddess or lamp,
turgescent tower, immobile love, life lives.
You navigate with me, my inmate until the day
they let fall what I am in the spray.

[A.K.]

La noche marina

Noche marina, estatua blanca y verde,
te amo, duerme conmigo. Fui por todas
las calles calcinándome y muriendo,
creció conmigo la madera, el hombre
conquistó su ceniza y se dispuso
a descansar rodeado por la tierra.

Cerró la noche para que tus ojos
no vieran su reposo miserable:
quiso proximidad, abrió los brazos
custodiado por seres y por muros,
y cayó al sueño del silencio, bajando
a tierra funeral con sus raíces.
Yo, noche Océano, a tu forma abierta,
a tu extensión que Aldebarán vigila,
a la boca mojada de tu canto
llegué con el amor que me construye.

Te vi, noche del mar, cuando nacías
golpeada por el nácar infinito:
vi tejerse las hebras estrelladas
y la electricidad de tu cintura
y el movimiento azul de los sonidos
que acosan tu dulzura devorada.

Ámame sin amor, sangrienta esposa.

Ámame con espacio, con el río
de tu respiración, con el aumento
de todos tus diamantes desbordados:
ámame sin la tregua de tu rostro,
dame la rectitud de tu quebranto.

Hermosa eres, amada, noche hermosa:
guardas la tempestad como una abeja
dormida en tus estambres alarmados,
y sueño y agua tiemblan en las copas
de tu pecho acosado de vertientes.

The Marine Night

Marine night, white and green statue,
I love you: sleep with me. I went through all
the streets, disintegrating and dying,
the wood grew with me, man
vanquished his ashes and got ready
to rest surrounded by the earth.

Night fell so that your eyes
might not see his wretched repose:
desiring to be close, he opened his arms
guarded by beings and walls,
and fell into the dream of silence, descending
with his roots into funereal land.
I, Oceanic night, arrived with the love that makes me,
and reached your open form, the vastness that Aldebaran
watches over, the wet mouth of your song.

I saw you, night of the sea, as you were born,
bruised by infinite mother-of-pearl:
I watched the starry threads weaving
and the electricity of your girdle
and the blue motion of the sounds
that harass your devoured sweetness.

Love me without love, ravaged wife.

Love me with space, with the river
of your breathing, with all your
inundated diamonds magnified:
love me without trace of truce,
give me the rightness of your refraction.

You're lovely, beloved, lovely night:
you hold the storm like a bee
asleep in the stamens of your alarm,
and water and sleep tremble in the glasses
of your bosom hemmed by valleys.

Nocturno amor, seguí lo que elevabas,
tu eternidad, la torre temblorosa
que asume las estrellas, la medida
de tu vacilación, las poblaciones
que levanta la espuma en tus costados:
estoy encadenado a tu garganta
y a los labios que rompes en la arena.

Quién eres? Noche de los mares, dime
si tu escarpada cabellera cubre
toda la soledad, si es infinito
este espacio de sangre y de praderas.
Dime quién eres, llena de navíos,
llena de lunas que tritura el viento,
dueña de todos los metales, rosa
de la profundidad, rosa mojada
por la intemperie del amor desnudo.

Túnica de la tierra, estatua verde,
dame una ola como una campana,
dame una ola de azahar furioso,
la multitud de hogueras, los navíos
del cielo capital, el agua en que navego,
la multitud del fuego celeste: quiero un solo
minuto de extensión y más que todos
los sueños, tu distancia:
toda la púrpura que mides, el grave
pensativo sistema constelado:
toda tu cabellera que visita
la oscuridad, y el día que preparas.

Quiero tener tu frente simultánea,
abrirla en mi interior para nacer
en todas tus orillas, ir ahora
con todos los secretos respirados,
con tus oscuras líneas resguardadas
en mí como la sangre o las banderas,
llevando estas secretas proporciones
al mar de cada día, a los combates
que en cada puerta – amores y amenazas –
viven dormidos.
                    Pero entonces

Nocturnal love, I followed where you rose,
your eternity, the swaying tower
that assumes the stars, the measure
of your vacillation, the settlements
raised on your flanks by the spray:
I'm chained to your throat
and to the lips you wreak on the sand.

Who are you? Night of the seas, tell me
whether your rugged head of hair covers
the whole of solitude, whether this expanse
of blood and pastures is infinite.
Tell me: who are you, filled with ships,
covered with moons pulverized by the wind,
owner of all metals, rose
of the deep, rose wet
with the weather of naked love.

Tunic of the earth, green statue,
give me a bell-like wave,
give me a wave full of wild scent,
the multiplicity of bonfires, the ships
of the capital heaven, the water on which I sail,
the multitude of celestial fire: I want a single
minute of extension and, more than all
dreams, your distance:
the width of the purple you measure, the grave
meditative system of the constellations:
all your hair visited
by the dark, and the day you make ready.

I want your sudden brow,
to open it up inside me so as to be born
on all your shores, go now
with all secrets breathed,
your dark lines harboured
in me like blood or flags,
carrying these secret proportions
to each day's sea, to the battles
that in each portal – loves and threats –
lie sleeping.
              But then

entraré en la ciudad con tantos ojos
como los tuyos, y sostendré la vestidura
con que me visitaste, y que me toquen
hasta el agua total que no se mide:
pureza y destrucción contra toda la muerte,
distancia que no puede gastarse, música
para los que duermen y para los que despiertan.

I shall enter the city with as many eyes
as you have, and I shall hold up the vesture
in which you visited me, and let myself be touched
as high as the total water which is measureless:
purity and destruction against all death,
distance that is unexpendable, music
for those that sleep and for those that wake.

[A.K.]

El vino

Vino de primavera . . . Vino de otoño, dadme
mis compañeros, una mesa en que caigan
hojas equinocciales, y el gran río del mundo
que palidezca un poco moviendo su sonido
lejos de nuestros cantos.
                              Soy buen compañero.

   No entraste en esta casa para que te arrancara
   un pedazo de ser. Tal vez cuando te vayas
   te lleves algo mío, castañas, rosas o
   una seguridad de raíces o naves
   que quise compartir contigo, compañero.

Canta conmigo hasta que las copas
se derramen dejando púrpura desprendida
sobre la mesa.
                    Esa miel viene a tu boca
desde la tierra, desde sus oscuros racimos.

   Cuántos me faltan, sombras del canto,
                                    compañeros
   que amé dando la frente, sacando de mi vida
   la incomparable ciencia varonil que profeso,
   la amistad, arboleda de rugosa ternura.

   Dame la mano, encuéntrate conmigo,
   simple, no busques nada en mis palabras
   sino la emanación de una planta desnuda.

Por qué me pides más que a un obrero? Ya sabes
que a golpes fui forjando mi enterrada herrería,
y que no quiero hablar sino como es mi lengua.
Sal a buscar doctores si no te gusta el viento.

Nosotros cantaremos con el vino fragoso
de la tierra: golpearemos las copas del Otoño,
y la guitarra o el silencio irán trayendo
líneas de amor, lenguaje de ríos que no existen,
estrofas adoradas que no tienen sentido.

Wine

Fall wine or spring wine, wine
and drinking mates, at a table littered
with leaves from the equinox, the Big River
of the world blanching to be so far
from our song.
           I'm an easy drinker.

You didn't come here so I could tear off
a piece of your life. When you leave
you can take something of mine: some roses or
chestnuts or surefire roots
to be shared with a comrade.

You can sing along with me until
our drinks run over and stain the board
purple.
          This mead for your mouth
comes straight from dusty clusters.

How many shades of my song are gone:
                       old comrades
I loved face to face, distilling from life
the virile science I profess:
amity, grove of rugged tenderness.

Give me your hand, come with me
simply and look for nothing in my words
beyond what comes or exudes from a plant.

Why ask me more than a workman? You know
I forged my buried smithy stroke-by-stroke
and don't care to speak except with my tongue.
Go look for doctors if you can't stand the wind.

O let's sing the rough wine of the earth,
beat the board with the glasses of fall,
while either a guitar or the silence go on bringing us
love-lines, the language of nonexistent rivers
or adorable stanzas with no sense at all.

                                                     [A. K.]

from *Odas elementales* (1954)

Oda al tomate

La calle
se llenó de tomates,
mediodía,
verano,
la luz
se parte
en dos
mitades
de tomate,
corre
por las calles
el jugo.
En diciembre
se desata
el tomate,
invade
las cocinas,
entra por los almuerzos,
se sienta
reposado
en los aparadores,
entre los vasos,
las mantequilleras,
los saleros azules.
Tiene
luz propia,
majestad benigna.
Debemos, por desgracia,
asesinarlo:
se hunde
el cuchillo
en su pulpa viviente,
es una roja
víscera,
un sol
fresco,
profundo,
inagotable,
llena las ensaladas

Ode to the Tomato

The street
drowns in tomatoes:
noon,
summer,
light
breaks
in two
tomato
halves,
and the streets
run
with juice.
In December
the tomato
cuts loose,
invades
kitchens,
takes over lunches,
settles
at rest
on sideboards,
with the glasses,
butter dishes,
blue salt-cellars.
It has
its own radiance,
a goodly majesty.
Too bad we must
assassinate:
a knife
plunges
into its living pulp,
red
viscera,
a fresh,
deep,
inexhaustible
sun
floods the salads

de Chile,
se casa alegremente
con la clara cebolla,
y para celebrarlo
se deja
caer
aceite,
hijo
esencial del olivo,
sobre sus hemisferios entreabiertos,
agrega
la pimienta
su fragancia,
la sal su magnetismo:
son las bodas
del día,
el perejil
levanta
banderines,
las papas
hierven vigorosamente,
el asado
golpea
con su aroma
en la puerta,
es hora!
vamos!
y sobre
la mesa, en la cintura
del verano,
el tomate,
astro de tierra,
estrella
repetida
y fecunda,
nos muestra
sus circunvoluciones,
sus canales,
la insigne plenitud
y la abundancia
sin hueso,
sin coraza,

of Chile,
beds cheerfully
with the blonde onion,
and to celebrate
oil
the filial essence
of the olive tree
lets itself fall
over its gaping hemispheres,
the pimento
adds
its fragrance,
salt its magnetism –
we have the day's
wedding:
parsley
flaunts
its little flags,
potatoes
thump to a boil,
the roasts
beat
down the door
with their aromas:
it's time!
let's go!
and upon
the table,
belted by summer,
tomatoes,
stars of the earth,
stars multiplied
and fertile
show off
their convolutions,
canals
and plenitudes
and the abundance
boneless,
without husk,

sin escamas ni espinas,
nos entrega
el regalo
de su color fogoso
y la totalidad de su frescura.

or scale or thorn,
grant us
the festival
of ardent colour
and all-embracing freshness.

[N.T.]

Oda al traje

Cada mañana esperas,
traje, sobre una silla
que te llene
mi vanidad, mi amor,
mi esperanza, mi cuerpo.
Apenas
salgo del sueño,
me despido del agua,
entro en tus mangas,
mis piernas buscan
el hueco de tus piernas
y así abrazado
por tu fidelidad infatigable
salgo a pisar el pasto,
entro en la poesía,
miro por las ventanas,
las cosas,
los hombres, las mujeres,
los hechos y las luchas
me van formando,
me van haciendo frente
labrándome las manos,
abriéndome los ojos,
gastándome la boca
y así,
traje,
yo también voy formándote,
sacándote los codos,
rompiéndote los hilos,
y así tu vida crece
a imagen de mi vida.
Al viento
ondulas y resuenas
como si fueras mi alma,
en los malos minutos
te adhieres
a mis huesos
vacíos, por la noche
la oscuridad, el sueño

Ode to the Clothes

Every morning you wait,
clothes, over a chair,
for my vanity,
my love,
my hope, my body
to fill you,
I have scarcely
left sleep,
I say goodbye to the water
and enter your sleeves,
my legs look for
the hollow of your legs,
and thus embraced
by your unwearying fidelity
I go out to tread the fodder,
I move into poetry,
I look through windows,
at things,
men, women,
actions and struggles
keep making me what I am,
opposing me,
employing my hands,
opening my eyes,
putting taste in my mouth,
and thus,
clothes,
I make you what you are,
pushing out your elbows,
bursting the seams,
and so your life swells
the image of my life.
You billow
and resound in the wind
as though you were my soul,
at bad moments
you cling
to my bones
empty, at night

pueblan con sus fantasmas
tus alas y las mías.
Yo pregunto
si un día
una bala
del enemigo
te dejara una mancha de mi sangre
y entonces
te morirás conmigo
o tal vez
no sea todo
tan dramático
sino simple,
y te irás enfermando,
traje,
conmigo,
envejeciendo
conmigo, con mi cuerpo
y juntos
entraremos
a la tierra.
Por eso
cada día
te saludo
con reverencia y luego
me abrazas y te olvido,
porque uno solo somos
y seguiremos siendo
frente al viento, en la noche,
las calles o la lucha
un solo cuerpo
tal vez, tal vez, alguna vez inmóvil.

the dark, sleep,
people with their phantoms
your wings and mine.
I ask
whether one day
a bullet
from the enemy
will stain you with my blood
and then
you will die with me
or perhaps
it may not be
so dramatic
but simple,
and you will sicken gradually,
clothes,
with me, with my body
and together
we will enter
the earth.
At the thought of this
every day
I greet you
with reverence, and then
you embrace me and I forget you
because we are one
and will go on facing
the wind together, at night,
the streets or the struggle,
one body,
maybe, maybe, one day motionless.

[W.S.M.]

from *Estravagario* (1958)

Y cuánto vive?

Cuánto vive el hombre, por fin?

Vive mil días o uno solo?

Una semana o varios siglos?

Por cuánto tiempo muere el hombre?

Qué quiere decir 'Para Siempre'?

Preocupado por este asunto
me dediqué a aclarar las cosas.

Busqué a los sabios sacerdotes,
los esperé después del rito,
los aceché cuando salían
a visitar a Dios y al Diablo.

Se aburrieron con mis preguntas.
Ellos tampoco sabían mucho,
eran sólo administradores.

Los médicos me recibieron,
entre una consulta y otra,
con un bisturí en cada mano,
saturados de aureomicina,
más ocupados cada día.
Según supe por lo que hablaban
el problema era como sigue:
nunca murió tanto microbio,
toneladas de ellos caían,
pero los pocos que quedaron
se manifestaban perversos.

Me dejaron tan asustado
que busqué a los enterradores.
Me fuí a los ríos donde queman
grandes cadáveres pintados,
pequeños muertos huesudos,

And How Long?

How long does a man live, after all?

Does he live a thousand days, or one only?

A week, or several centuries?

How long does a man spend dying?

What does it mean to say 'for ever'?

Lost in these preoccupations,
I set myself to clear things up.

I sought out knowledgeable priests,
I waited for them after their rituals,
I watched them when they went their ways
to visit God and the Devil.

They wearied of my questions.
They on their part knew very little;
they were no more than administrators.

Medical men received me
in between consultations,
a scalpel in each hand,
saturated in aureomycin,
busier each day.
As far as I could tell from their talk,
the problem was as follows:
it was not so much the death of a microbe —
they went down by the ton —
but the few which survived
showed signs of perversity.

They left me so startled
that I sought out the grave-diggers.
I went to the rivers where they burn
enormous painted corpses,
tiny bony bodies,

emperadores recubiertos
por escamas aterradoras,
mujeres aplastadas de pronto
por una ráfaga de cólera.
Eran riberas de difuntos
y especialistas cenicientos.

Cuando llegó mi oportunidad
les largué unas cuantas preguntas,
ellos me ofrecieren quemarme:
era todo lo que sabían.

En mi país los enterradores
me contestaron, entre copas:
– 'Búscate una moza robusta,
y déjate de tonterías.'

Nunca vi gentes tan alegres.

Cantaban levantando el vino
por la salud y por la muerte.
Eran grandes fornicadores.

Regresé a mi casa más viejo
después de recorrer el mundo.

No le pregunto a nadie nada.

Pero sé cada día menos.

emperors with an aura
of terrible curses,
women snuffed out at a stroke
by a wave of cholera.
There were whole beaches of dead
and ashy specialists.

When I got the chance
I asked them a slew of questions.
They offered to burn me;
it was the only thing they knew.

In my own country the undertakers
answered me, between drinks:
'Get yourself a good woman
and give up this nonsense.'

I never saw people so happy.

Raising their glasses they sang,
toasting health and death.
They were huge fornicators.

I returned home, much older
after crossing the world.

Now I question nobody.

But I know less every day.

[A.R.]

Fábula de la sirena y los borrachos

Todos estos señores estaban dentro
cuando ella entró completamente desnuda
ellos habían bebido y comenzaron a escupirla
ella no entendía nada recién salía del río
era una sirena que se había extraviado
los insultos corrían sobre su carne lisa
la inmundicia cubrió sus pechos de oro
ella no sabía llorar por eso no lloraba
no sabía vestirse por eso no se vestía
la tatuaron con cigarrillos y con corchos quemados
y reían hasta caer al suelo de la taberna
ella no hablaba porque no sabía hablar
sus ojos eran color de amor distante
sus brazos construídos de topacios gemelos
sus labios se cortaron en la luz del coral
y de pronto salió por esa puerta
apenas entró al río quedó limpia
relució como una piedra blanca en la lluvia
y sin mirar atrás nadó de nuevo
nadó hacia nunca más hacia morir.

Fable of the Mermaid and the Drunks

All these men were there inside
when she entered, utterly naked.
They had been drinking, and began to spit at her.
Recently come from the river, she understood nothing.
She was a mermaid who had lost her way.
The taunts flowed over her glistening flesh.
Obscenities drenched her golden breasts.
A stranger to tears, she did not weep.
A stranger to clothes, she did not dress.
They pocked her with cigarette ends and with burnt corks,
and rolled on the tavern floor with laughter.
She did not speak, since speech was unknown to her.
Her eyes were the colour of faraway love,
her arms were matching topazes.
Her lips moved soundlessly in coral light,
and ultimately she left by that door.
Scarcely had she entered the river than she was cleansed,
gleaming once more like a white stone in the rain;
and without a backward look, she swam once more,
swam toward nothingness, swam to her dying.

[A.R.]

Demasiados nombres

Se enreda el lunes con el martes
y la semana con el año:
no se puede cortar el tiempo
con tus tijeras fatigadas,
y todos los nombres del día
los borra el agua de la noche.

Nadie puede llamarse Pedro,
ninguna es Rosa ni María,
todos somos polvo o arena,
todos somos lluvia en la lluvia.
Me han hablado de Venezuelas,
de Paraguayes y de Chiles,
no sé de lo que están hablando:
conozco la piel de la tierra
y sé que no tiene apellido.

Cuando viví con las raíces
me gustaron más que las flores,
y cuando hablé con una piedra
sonaba como una campana.

Es tan larga la primavera
que dura todo el invierno:
el tiempo perdió los zapatos:
un año tiene cuatro siglos.

Cuando duermo todas las noches,
cómo me llamo o no me llamo?
Y cuando me despierto quién soy
si no era yo cuando dormía?

Esto quiere decir que apenas
desembarcamos en la vida,
que venimos recién naciendo,
que no nos llenemos la boca
con tantos nombres inseguros,
con tantas etiquetas tristes,
con tantas letras rimbombantes,

Too Many Names

Mondays are meshed with Tuesdays
and the week with the whole year.
Time cannot be cut
with your exhausted scissors,
and all the names of the day
are washed out by the waters of night.

No one can claim the name of Pedro,
nobody is Rosa or María,
all of us are dust or sand,
all of us are rain under rain.
They have spoken to me of Venezuelas,
of Chiles and Paraguays;
I have no idea what they are saying.
I know only the skin of the earth
and I know it has no name.

When I lived amongst the roots
they pleased me more than flowers did,
and when I spoke to a stone
it rang like a bell.

It is so long, the spring
which goes on all winter.
Time lost its shoes.
A year lasts four centuries.

When I sleep every night,
what am I called or not called?
And when I wake, who am I
if I was not I while I slept?

This means to say that scarcely
have we landed into life
than we come as if new-born;
let us not fill our mouths
with so many faltering names,
with so many sad formalities,
with so many pompous letters,

con tanto tuyo y tanto mío,
con tanta firma en los papeles.

Yo pienso confundir las cosas,
unirlas y recién nacerlas,
entreverarlas, desve stirlas,
hasta que la luz del mundo
tenga la unidad del océano,
una integridad generosa,
una fragancia crepitante.

with so much of yours and mine,
with so much signing of papers.

I have a mind to confuse things,
unite them, make them new-born,
mix them up, undress them,
until all light in the world
has the oneness of the ocean,
a generous, vast wholeness,
a crackling, living fragrance.

[A.R.]

from *Testamento de otoño*

FINAL-
MENTE SE
DIRIGE CON
ARROBA-
MIENTO A
SU AMADA

Matilde Urrutia, aquí te dejo
lo que tuve y lo que no tuve,
lo que soy y lo que no soy.
Mi amor es un niño que llora,
no quiere salir de tus brazos,
yo te lo dejo para siempre:
eres para mí la más bella.

Eres para mí la más bella,
la más tatuada por el viento,
como un arbolito del sur,
como un avellano en agosto,
eres para mí suculenta
como una panadería,
es de tierra tu corazón
pero tus manos son celestes.

Eres roja y eres picante,
eres blanca y eres salada
como escabeche de cebolla,
eres un piano que ríe
con todas las notas del alma
y sobre mí cae la música
de tus pestañas y tu pelo,
me baño en tu sombra de oro
y me deleitan tus orejas
como si las hubiera visto
en las mareas de coral:
por tus uñas luché en las olas
contra pescados pavorosos.

De Sur a Sur se abren tus ojos,
y de Este a Oeste tu sonrisa,
no se te pueden ver los pies,
y el sol se entretiene estrellando
el amanecer en tu pelo.
Tu cuerpo y tu rostro llegaron
como yo, de regiones duras,
de ceremonias lluviosas,

from *Autumn Testament*

FINALLY HE
ADDRESSES
HIMSELF
ECSTATIC-
ALLY TO
HIS
BELOVED

Matilde Urrutia, I leave you here
what I had and did not have,
what I am and what I'm not.
My love is a child crying
afraid to leave your arms,
I leave him to you for ever:
you, most beautiful of women.

You are the one most beautiful,
the wind has most tattooed
like a little southern tree,
like a hazel tree in August,
you are as succulent for me
as a baker's full of bread,
your heart is made of earth
but your hands are celestial.

You are red and you are hot,
you are white and very salty
like a laurel sauce with onions,
you are a piano laughing
with all the notes your soul,
your eyelids and your hair,
consent to shed on me,
I bathe in your golden shadow
and your ears delight me
as if I had found them
in the pools of coral reefs:
for your fingernails I fought
with terrifying fish.

From South to South your eyes,
from East to West your smile –
one cannot see your feet,
the sun's delightful stars
dawn in your hair.
Body and face arrived
like me from angry regions,
from rainy rituals,

de antiguas tierras y martirios,
sigue cantando el Bío-Bío
en nuestra arcilla ensangrentada,
pero tú trajiste del bosque,
todos los secretos perfumes
y esa manera de lucir
un perfil de flecha perdida,
una medalla de guerrero.
Tú fuiste mi vencedora
por el amor y por la tierra,
porque tu boca me traía
antepasados manantiales,
citas en bosque de otra edad,
oscuros tambores mojados:
de pronto oí que me llamaban:
era de lejos y de cuando:
me acerqué al antiguo follaje
y besé mi sangre en tu boca,
corazón mío, mi araucana.

Qué puedo dejarte si tienes,
Matilde Urrutia, en tu contacto
ese aroma de hojas quemadas,
esa fragancia de frutillas
y entre tus dos pechos marinos
el crepúsculo de Cauquenes
y el olor de peumo de Chile?

Es el alto otoño del mar
lleno de niebla y cavidades.
la tierra se extiende y respira,
se le caen al mes las hojas.
Y tu inclinada en mi trabajo
con tu pasión y tu paciencia
deletreando las patas verdes,
las telarañas, los insectos
de mi mortal caligrafía,
oh leona de pies pequeñitos,
qué haría sin tus manos breves?
dónde andaría caminando
sin corazón y sin objeto?

old earths and martyrdoms,
the Bío-Bío sings
along our blood-soaked clay
but you brought out of jungles
every secret aroma
and that manner of shining,
the profile of lost arrows,
a warrior's medallion.
You were my vanquisher
for love and for the earth
because your mouth engendered
ancestral lineages,
meetings in ancient forests,
dark, humid drums
I suddenly hear calling:
it was from far, I know not when,
I touched the age-old foliage,
kissing my blood in your mouth,
my heart, my Araucanian girl.

What can I leave you, Matilde Urrutia,
if in your touch you own
that perfume of burned leaves,
that strawberry fragrance,
and between your breasts
the sea-dusk of Cauquenes,
the laurel smell of Chile?

It is high autumn on the sea,
season of mists and cavities,
the earth stretches and breathes,
the leaves fall month by month.
And you, leaning into my work,
with your passion, with your patience,
deciphering green batons,
the spider webs, the insects
of my mortal calligraphy,
oh lioness of the small feet
what would I do without your brief hands?
where would I go, where would I travel
deprived of heart and aim?

en qué lejanos autobuses,
enfermo de fuego o de nieve?

Te debo el otoño marino
con la humedad de las raíces,
y la niebla como una uva,
y el sol silvestre y elegante:
te debo este cajón callado
en que se pierden los dolores
y sólo suben a la frente
las corolas de la alegría.
Todo te lo debo a ti,
tórtola desencadenada,
mi codorniza copetona,
mi jilguero de las montañas,
mi campesina de Coihueco.

Alguna vez si ya no somos,
si ya no vamos ni venimos
bajo siete capas de polvo
y los pies secos de la muerte,
estaremos juntos, amor,
extrañamente confundidos.
Nuestras espinas diferentes,
nuestros ojos maleducados,
nuestros pies que no se encontraban
y nuestros besos indelebles,
todo estará por fin reunido,
pero de qué nos servirá
la unidad en un cementerio?
Que no nos separe la vida
y se vaya al diablo la muerte!

in what far buses
fevered with fire or snow?

I owe you autumn by the sea,
with the dankness of roots
and the mist like a grape
and the elegant country sun:
I owe you this silent valley
in which sorrows are lost
and only joy's corollas
rise to the forehead.
I owe you everything,
my dove unleashed,
aristocratic quail,
linnet of the mountains,
my peasant princess from Coihueco.

Some time if we're not yet,
if we're not gone, if we're not coming,
under seven layers of dust
and death's dry footsteps,
we'll be together, love,
strangely confused together.
Our separate spines,
our cheeky eyes,
our feet which never met,
our indelible kisses,
will all come together in the end –
but what will be the use
of graveyard unity? Let life not part us
and to hell with death!

[N.T.]

from *Las piedras de Chile* (1961)

El león

Un gran león llegó de lejos:
era grande como el silencio,
tenía sed, buscaba sangre,
y detrás de su investidura
tenía fuego como una casa,
ardía como un monte de Osorno.

No encontró más que soledad.
Rugió de huraño, de hambriento:
sólo podía comer aire,
espuma impune de la costa,
heladas lechugas del mar,
aire de color de pájaro,
inaceptables alimentos.

Triste león de otro planeta
traído por la alta marea
a los islotes de Isla Negra,
al archipiélago de sal,
sin más que un hocico vacío,
unas garras desocupadas
y una cola como un plumero.

Fue sintiendo todo el ridículo
de su contextura marcial
y con los años que pasaban
se fue arrugando de vergüenza.
La timidez lo llevó entonces
a las arrogancias peores
y fue envejeciendo como uno
de los leones de la plaza,
se fue convirtiendo en adorno
de escalinata, de jardín,
hasta enterrar le triste frente,
clavar los ojos en la lluvia,
y quedarse quieto esperando
la justicia gris de la piedra,
la hora de la geología.

The Lion

A great lion came from the distances.
It was huge as silence is,
it was thirsty, it was after blood,
and behind its posturing
it had fire, as a house has,
it burned like a mountain of Osorno.

It found only solitude,
it roared, out of uncertainty and hunger –
the only thing to eat was air,
the wild foam of the coast,
frozen sea lettuces,
air the colour of birds,
unacceptable nourishment.

Wistful lion from another planet,
cast up by the high tide
on the rocky coast of Isla Negra,
the salty archipelago,
with nothing more than an empty maw,
claws that were idle
and a tail like a feather duster.

It was well aware of the foolishness
of its aggressive appearance
and with the passing of years
it wrinkled up in shame.
Its timidity led it on
to worse displays of arrogance
and it went on ageing like one
of the lions in the Plaza,
it slowly turned into an ornament
for a portico or a garden,
to the point of hiding its sad forehead,
fixing its eyes on the rain
and keeping still to wait for
the grey justice of stone,
its geological hour.

[A.R.]

El retrato en la roca

Yo sí lo conocí, viví los años
con él, con su substancia de oro y piedra,
era un hombre cansado:
dejó en el Paraguay su padre y madre,
sus hijos, sus sobrinos.
sus últimos cuñados,
su puerta, sus gallinas,
y algunos libros entreabiertos.
Llamaron a la puerta.
Cuando abrió lo sacó la policía,
y lo apalearon tanto
que escupió sangre en Francia, en Dinamarca,
en España, en Italia, trajinando,
y así murió y dejé de ver su cara,
dejé de oír su hondísimo silencio,
cuando una vez, de noche con chubasco,
con nieve que tejía
el traje puro de la cordillera,
a caballo, allá lejos,
miré y allí estaba mi amigo:
de piedra era su rostro,
su perfil desafiaba la intemperie,
en su nariz quebraba el viento
un largo aullido de hombre perseguido:
allí vino a parar el desterrado:
vive en su patria convertido en piedra.

The Portrait in the Rock

Oh yes I knew him, I spent years with him,
with his golden and stony substance,
he was a man who was tired –
in Paraguay he left his father and mother,
his sons, his nephews,
his latest in-laws,
his house, his chickens,
and some half-opened books.
They called him to the door.
When he opened it, the police took him,
and they beat him up so much
that he spat blood in France, in Denmark,
in Spain, in Italy, moving about,
and so he died and I stopped seeing his face,
stopped hearing his profound silence;
then once, on a night of storms,
with snow spreading
a smooth cloak on the mountains,
on horseback, there, far off,
I looked and there was my friend –
his face was formed in stone,
his profile defied the wild weather,
in his nose the wind was muffling
the moaning of the persecuted.
There the exile came to ground.
Changed into stone, he lives in his own country.

[A. R.]

from *Cantos ceremoniales* (1961)

Fin de fiesta

XII

Espuma blanca, marzo en la Isla, veo
trabajar ola y ola, quebrarse la blancura,
desbordar el océano de su insaciable copa,
el cielo estacionario dividido
por largos lentos vuelos de aves sacerdotales
y llega el amarillo,
cambia el color del mes, crece la barba
del otoño marino,
y yo me llamo Pablo,
soy el mismo hasta ahora,
tengo amor, tengo dudas,
tengo deudas,
tengo el inmenso mar con empleados
que mueven ola y ola,
tengo tanta intemperie que visito
naciones no nacidas:
voy y vengo del mar y sus países,
conozco
los idiomas de la espina,
el diente del pez duro,
escalofrío de las latitudes,
la sangre del coral, la taciturna
noche de la ballena,
porque de tierra en tierra fui avanzando
estuario, insufribles territorios,
y siempre regresé, no tuve paz:
qué podía decir sin mis raíces?

XIII

Qué podía decir sin tocar tierra?
A quién me dirigía sin la lluvia?
Por eso nunca estuve donde estuve
y no navegué más que de regreso
y de las catedrales no guardé
retrato ni cabellos: he tratado
de fundar piedra mía a plena mano,

Fiesta's End

XII

White foam, March in Isla Negra, I see
wave working on wave, the whiteness weakening,
the ocean overflowing from its bottomless cup,
the still sky crisscrossed
by long slow flights of sacerdotal birds,
and the yellow comes,
the month changes colour, the beard
of a sea-coast autumn grows,
and I am called Pablo,
I am the same so far,
I have love, I have doubts,
I have debts.
I have the vast sea with its workers
moving wave after wave,
I am so restless that I visit
nations not yet born –
I come and go on the sea and its countries,
I know
the language of the fishbone,
the tooth of the hard fish,
chill of the latitudes,
blood of the coral, the silent
night of the whale,
for from land to land I went, exploring
estuaries, insufferable regions,
and always I returned, I found no peace –
what could I say at all without my roots?

XIII

What could I say without coming to ground?
To whom would I turn without the rain?
Thus I was never where I found myself
and I took no journey other than the return
and I kept neither picture nor lock of hair
from the cathedrals – I have tried
to shape my own stone with the work of my hands,

con razón, sin razón, con desvarío,
con furia y equilibrio: a toda hora
toqué los territorios del león
y la torre intranquila de la abeja,
por eso cuando vi lo que ya había visto
y toqué tierra y lodo, piedra y espuma mía,
seres que reconocen mis pasos, mi palabra,
plantas ensortijadas que besaban mi boca,
dije: 'aquí estoy', me desnudé en la luz,
dejé caer las manos en el mar,
y cuando todo estaba transparente,
bajo la tierra, me quedé tranquilo.

sensibly, wildly, following my whim,
with rage and equilibrium – at every hour
I touched the territories of the lion,
the restless sanctuary of the bees,
thus, when I saw what I had already seen
and touched both earth and mud, stone and my foam,
natures which recognize my steps, my words,
curling plants which kissed my mouth,
I said 'I am here', I stripped in the light,
I let my hands fall to the sea,
and when everything took on transparency,
under the land, I was at peace.

[A. R.]

from *Plenos poderes* (1962)

La palabra

Nació
la palabra en la sangre,
creció en el cuerpo oscuro, palpitando,
y voló con los labios y la boca.

Más lejos y más cerca
aún, aún venía
de padres muertos y de errantes razas,
de territorios que se hicieron piedra,
que se cansaron de sus pobres tribus,
porque cuando el dolor salió al camiño
los pueblos anduvieron y llegaron
y nueva tierra y agua reunieron
para sembrar de nuevo su palabra.
Y así la herencia es ésta:
éste es el aire que nos comunica
con el hombre enterrado y con la aurora
de nuevos seres que aún no amanecieron.

Aún la atmósfera tiembla
con la primera palabra
elaborada
con pánico y gemido.
Salió
de las tinieblas
y hasta ahora no hay trueno
que truene aún con su ferretería
como aquella palabra,
la primera
palabra pronunciada:
tal vez sólo un susurro fue, una gota,
y cae y cae aún su catarata.

Luego el sentido llena la palabra.
Quedó preñada y se llenó de vidas.
Todo fue nacimientos y sonidos:
la afirmación, la claridad, la fuerza,
la negación, la destrucción, la muerte:
el verbo asumió todos los poderes

The Word

The word
was born in the blood,
grew in the dark body, beating,
and flew through the lips and the mouth.

Farther away and nearer
still, still it came
from dead fathers and from wandering races,
from lands that had returned to stone,
weary of their poor tribes,
because when pain took to the roads,
the settlements set out and arrived
and new lands and water reunited
to sow their word anew.
And so, this is the inheritance –
this is the wavelength which connects us
with the dead man and the dawn
of new beings not yet come to light.

Still the atmosphere quivers
with the initial word
dressed up
in terror and sighing.
It emerged
from the darkness
and until now there is no thunder
that rumbles yet with all the iron
of that word,
the first
word uttered –
perhaps it was only a ripple, a drop,
and yet its great cataract falls and falls.

Later on, the word fills with meaning.
It remained gravid and it filled up with lives.
Everything had to do with births and sounds –
affirmation, clarity, strength,
negation, destruction, death –
the verb took over all the power

y se fundió existencia con esencia
en la electricidad de su hermosura.

Palabra humana, sílaba, cadera
de larga luz y dura platería,
hereditaria copa que recibe
las comunicaciones de la sangre:
he aquí que el silencio fue integrado
por el total de la palabra humana
y no hablar es morir entre los seres:
se hace lenguaje hasta la cabellera,
habla la boca sin mover los labios:
los ojos de repente son palabras.

Yo tomo la palabra y la recorro
como si fuera sólo forma humana,
me embelesan sus líneas y navego
en cada resonancia del idioma:
pronuncio y soy y sin hablar me acerca
al fin de las palabras al silencio.

Bebo por la palabra levantando
una palabra o copa cristalina,
en ella bebo
el vino del idioma
o el agua interminable,
manantial maternal de las palabras,
y copa y agua y vino
originan mi canto
porque el verbo es origen
y vierte vida: es sangre,
es la sangre que expresa su substancia
y está dispuesto así su desarrollo:
dan cristal al cristal, sangre a la sangre,
y dan vida a la vida las palabras.

and blended existence with essence
in the electricity of its beauty.

Human word, syllable, combination
of spread light and the fine art of the silversmith,
hereditary goblet which gathers
the communications of the blood –
here is where silence was gathered up
in the completeness of the human word
and, for human beings, not to speak is to die –
language extends even to the hair,
the mouth speaks without the lips moving –
all of a sudden the eyes are words.

I take the word and go over it
as though it were nothing more than a human shape,
its arrangements awe me and I find my way
through each variation in the spoken word –
I utter and I am and without speaking I approach
the limit of words and the silence.

I drink to the word, raising
a word or a shining cup,
in it I drink
the pure wine of language
or inexhaustible water,
maternal source of words,
and cup and water and wine
give rise to my song
because the verb is the source
and vivid life – it is blood,
blood which expresses its substance
and so implies its own unwinding –
words give glass-quality to glass, blood to blood,
and life to life itself.

[A.R.]

El pueblo

De aquel hombre me acuerdo y no han pasado
sino dos siglos desde que lo vi,
no anduvo ni a caballo ni en carroza:
a puro pie
deshizo
las distancias
y no llevaba espada ni armadura,
sino redes al hombro,
hacha o martillo o pala,
nunca apaleó a ninguno de su especie:
su hazaña fue contra el agua o la tierra,
contra el trigo para que hubiera pan,
contra el árbol gigante para que diera leña,
contra los muros para abrir las puertas,
contra la arena construyendo muros
y contra el mar para hacerlo parir.

Lo conocí y aún no se me borra.

Cayeron en pedazos las carrozas,
la guerra destruyó puertas y muros,
la ciudad fue un puñado de cenizas,
se hicieron polvo todos los vestidos,
y él para mí subsiste,
sobrevive en la arena,
cuando antes parecía
todo imborrable menos él.

En el ir y venir de las familias
a veces fue mi padre o mi pariente
o apenas si era él o si no era
tal vez aquel que no volvió a su casa
porque el agua o la tierra lo tragaron
o lo mató una máquina o un árbol
o fue aquel enlutado carpintero
que iba detrás del ataúd, sin lágrimas,
alguien en fin que no tenía nombre,
que se llamaba metal o madera,
y a quien miraron otros desde arriba

The People

That man I remember well, and at least two centuries
have passed since I saw him:
he travelled neither on horseback nor in a carriage –
purely on foot
he undid
the distances,
carrying neither sword nor weapon
but nets on his shoulder,
axe or hammer or spade;
he never fought with another of his kind –
his struggle was with water or with earth,
with the wheat, for it to become bread,
with the towering tree, for it to yield wood,
with the walls, to open doors in them,
with the sand, constructing walls,
and with the sea, to make it bear fruit.

I knew him and still he is there in me.

The carriages splintered in pieces,
war destroyed doorways and walls,
the city was a fistful of ashes,
all the dresses withered into dust,
and he persists, for my sake,
he survives in the sand,
where everything previously
seemed durable except him.

In the comings and goings of families,
at times he was my father or my relative
or (it may have been, it may not)
perhaps the one who did not come home
because water or earth devoured him
or a machine or a tree killed him,
or he was that funeral carpenter
who walked behind the coffin, but dry-eyed,
someone who never had a name
except as wood or metal have,
and on whom others looked from above,

sin ver la hormiga
sino el hormiguero
y que cuando sus pies no se movían,
porque el pobre cansado había muerto,
no vieron nunca que no lo veían:
había ya otros pies en donde estuvo.

Los otros pies eran él mismo,
también las otras manos,
el hombre sucedía:
cuando ya parecía transcurrido
era el mismo de nuevo,
allí estaba otra vez cavando tierra,
cortando tela, pero sin camisa,
allí estaba y no estaba, como entonces,
se había ido y estaba de nuevo,
y como nunca tuvo cementerio,
ni tumba, ni su nombre fue grabado
sobre la piedra que cortó sudando,
nunca sabía nadie que llegaba
y nadie supo cuando se moría,
así es que sólo cuando el pobre pudo
resucitó otra vez sin ser notado.

Era el hombre sin duda, sin herencia,
sin vaca, sin bandera,
y no se distinguía entre los otros,
los otros que eran él,
desde arriba era gris como el subsuelo,
como el cuero era pardo,
era amarillo cosechando trigo,
era negro debajo de la mina,
era color de piedra en el castillo,
en el barco pesquero era color de atún
y color de caballo en la pradera:
cómo podía nadie distinguirlo
si era el inseparable, el elemento,
tierra, carbón o mar vestido de hombre?

Donde vivió crecía
cuanto el hombre tocaba:
la piedra hostil,

unable to see
the ant for the ant-hill;
so that when his feet no longer moved
because, poor and tired, he had died,
they never saw what they were not used to seeing –
already other feet walked in his place.

The other feet were still him,
equally the other hands,
the man persisted –
when it seemed that now he was spent,
he was the same man over again,
there he was once more, tilling the soil,
cutting cloth, but without a shirt,
there he was and was not, as before,
he had gone and was back again,
and since he never had cemetery
nor tomb, nor his name engraved
on the stone that he sweated to cut,
nobody ever knew of his arrival,
and nobody knew when he died,
thus only when the poor man was able
did he come back to life again, unnoticed.

He was the man all right, without inheritance,
cattle or coat of arms,
and he did not stand out from the others,
the others who were himself,
from above he was grey like clay,
he was drab as leather,
he was yellow harvesting wheat,
he was black deep in the mine,
he was stone-coloured in the castle,
in the fishing boat, the colour of tunny,
horse-coloured in the meadow –
how could anyone distinguish him
if he were the wholeness, the element,
earth, coal or sea, in the guise of a man?

Where he lived, everything
a man touched would grow:
the hostile stones,

quebrada
por sus manos,
se convertía en orden
y una a una formaron
la recta claridad del edificio,
hizo el pan con sus manos,
movilizó los trenes,
se poblaron de pueblos las distancias,
otros hombres crecieron,
llegaron las abejas,
y porque el hombre crea y multiplica
la primavera caminó al mercado
entre panaderías y palomas.

El padre de los panes fue olvidado,
él que cortó y anduvo, machacando
y abriendo surcos, acarreando arena,
cuando todo existió ya no existía,
él daba su existencia, eso era todo.
Salió a otra parte a trabajar, y luego
se fue a morir rodando
como piedra del río:
aguas abajo lo llevó la muerte.

Yo, que lo conocí, lo vi bajando
hasta no ser sino lo que dejaba:
calles que apenas pudo conocer,
casas que nunca y nunca habitaría.

Y vuelvo a verlo, y cada día espero.

Lo veo en su ataúd y resurrecto.

Lo distingo entre todos
los que son sus iguales
y me parece que no puede ser,
que así no vamos a ninguna parte,
que suceder así no tiene gloria.

Yo creo que en el trono debe estar
este hombre, bien calzado y coronado.

hewn
by his hands,
took shape and form
and one by one took on
the sharp clarity of buildings,
he made bread with his hands,
set the trains running,
the distances bred townships,
other men grew up,
the bees arrived,
and through man's creating and multiplying,
spring wandered into the market place
between doves and bakeries.

The father of the loaves was forgotten,
he who cut and walked, beating
and opening paths, shifting sand,
when everything else existed, he existed no longer,
he gave away his existence, that was everything.
He went somewhere else to work and ultimately
he went into death, rolling
like a river stone –
death carried him off downstream.

I, who knew him, saw him go down
till he existed only in what he was leaving –
streets he could scarcely be aware of,
houses he never never would inhabit.

I come back to see him, and every day I wait.

I see him in his coffin and resurrected.

I pick him out from all
the others who are his equals
and it seems to me that it cannot be,
that in this way, we are going nowhere,
to survive so has no glory.

I believe that Heaven must include
that man, properly shod and crowned.

Creo que los que hicieron tantas cosas
deben ser dueños de todas las cosas.
Y los que hacen el pan deben comer!

Y deben tener luz los de la mina!

Basta ya de encadenados grises!

Basta de pálidos desaparecidos!

Ni un hombre más que pase sin que reine.

Ni una sola mujer sin su diadema.

Para todas las manos guantes de oro.

Frutas de sol a todos los oscuros!

Yo conocí aquel hombre y cuando pude,
cuando ya tuve ojos en la cara,
cuando ya tuve la voz en la boca
lo busqué entre las tumbas, y le dije
apretándole un brazo que aún no era polvo:

'Todos se irán, tú quedarás viviente,

Tú encendiste la vida.

Tú hiciste lo que es tuyo.'

Por eso nadie se moleste cuando
parece que estoy solo y no estoy solo,
no estoy con nadie y hablo para todos:

Alguien me está escuchando y no lo saben,
pero aquellos que canto y que lo saben
siguen naciendo y llenarán el mundo.

I think that those who made so many things
ought to be masters of everything.
And those who make bread ought to eat!

And those in the mine should have light!

Enough by now of grey men in chains!

Enough of the pale lost ones!

Not another man will go past except as a ruler.

Not a single woman without her diadem.

Gloves of gold for every hand.

Fruits of the sun for all the obscure ones!

I knew that man, and when I could,
when he still had eyes in his head,
when he still had a voice in his throat,
I sought him among the tombs, and I said to him,
pressing his arm that was still not dust:

'Everything will pass, and you will still be living.

You set fire to life.

You made what is yours.'

So let no one worry when
I seem to be alone and am not alone,
I am not with nobody and I speak for all –

Someone is listening to me and, although they do not know it,
those I sing of, those who know
go on being born and will fill up the world.

[A.R.]

from *Memorial de Isla Negra* (1964)

La poesía

Y fue a esa edad . . . Llegó la poesía
a buscarme. No sé, no sé de dónde
salió, de invierno o río.
No sé cómo ni cuándo,
no, no eran voces, no eran
palabras, ni silencio,
pero desde una calle me llamaba,
desde las ramas de la noche,
de pronto entre los otros,
entre fuegos violentos
o regresando solo,
allí estaba sin rostro
y me tocaba.

Yo no sabía qué decir, mi boca
no sabía
nombrar,
mis ojos eran ciegos,
y algo golpeaba en mi alma,
fiebre o alas perdidas.
y me fui haciendo solo,
descifrando
aquella quemadura,
y escribí la primera línea vaga,
vaga sin cuerpo, pura
tontería,
pura sabiduría
del que no sabe nada,
y vi de pronto
el cielo
desgranado
y abierto,
planetas,
plantaciones palpitantes,
la sombra perforada,
acribillada
por flechas, fuego y flores,
la noche arrolladora, el universo.

Poetry

And it was at that age . . . Poetry arrived
in search of me. I don't know, I don't know where
it came from, from winter or a river.
I don't know how or when,
no, they were not voices, they were not
words, nor silence,
but from a street I was summoned,
from the branches of night,
abruptly from the others,
among violent fires
or returning alone,
there I was without a face
and it touched me.

I did not know what to say, my mouth
had no way
with names,
my eyes were blind,
and something started in my soul,
fever or forgotten wings,
and I made my own way,
deciphering
that fire,
and I wrote the first faint line,
faint, without substance, pure
nonsense,
pure wisdom
of someone who knows nothing,
and suddenly I saw
the heavens
unfastened
and open,
planets,
palpitating plantations,
shadow perforated,
riddled
with arrows, fire and flowers,
the winding night, the universe.

Y yo, mínimo ser,
ebrio del gran vacío
constelado,
a semejanza, a imagen
del misterio,
me sentí parte pura
del abismo,
rodé con las estrellas,
mi corazón se desató en el viento.

And I, infinitesimal being,
drunk with the great starry
void,
likeness, image of
mystery,
felt myself a pure part
of the abyss,
I wheeled with the stars,
my heart broke loose on the wind.

[A.R.]

Religión en el este

Allí en Rangoon comprendí que los dioses
eran tan enemigos como Dios
del pobre ser humano.
                              Dioses
de alabastro tendidos
como ballenas blancas,
dioses dorados como las espigas,
dioses serpientes enroscados
al crimen de nacer,
budhas desnudos y elegantes
sonriendo en el cocktail
de la vacía eternidad
como Cristo en su cruz horrible,
todos dispuestos a todo,
a imponernos su cielo,
todos con llagas o pistola
para comprar piedad o quemarnos la sangre,
dioses feroces del hombre
para esconder la cobardía,
y allí todo era así,
toda la tierra olía a cielo,
a mercadería celeste.

Religion in the East

There in Rangoon I realized that the gods
were enemies, just like God,
of the poor human being.
                              Gods
in alabaster extended
like white whales,
gods gilded like spikes,
serpent gods entwining
the crime of being born,
naked and elegant buddhas
smiling at the cocktail party
of empty eternity
like Christ on his horrible cross,
all of them capable of anything,
of imposing on us their heaven,
all with torture or pistol
to purchase piety or burn our blood,
fierce gods made by men
to conceal their cowardice,
and there it was all like that,
the whole earth reeking of heaven,
and heavenly merchandise.

[A.R.]

Oh tierra, espérame

Vuélveme oh sol
a mi destino agreste,
lluvia del viejo bosque,
devuélveme el aroma y las espadas
que caían del cielo,
la solitaria paz de pasto y piedra,
la humedad de las márgenes del río,
el olor del alerce,
el viento vivo como un corazón
latiendo entre la huraña muchedumbre
de la gran araucaria.

Tierra, devuélveme tus dones puros,
las torres del silencio que subieron
de la solemnidad de sus raíces:
quiero volver a ser lo que no he sido,
aprender a volver desde tan hondo
que entre todas las cosas naturales
pueda vivir o no vivir: no importa
ser una piedra más, la piedra oscura,
la piedra pura que se lleva el río.

Oh Earth, Wait for Me

Return me, oh sun,
to my wild destiny,
rain of the ancient wood,
bring me back the aroma and the swords
that fall from the sky,
the solitary peace of pasture and rock,
the damp at the river-margins,
the smell of the larch tree,
the wind alive like a heart
beating in the crowded restlessness
of the towering araucaria.

Earth, give me back your pure gifts,
the towers of silence which rose
from the solemnity of their roots.
I want to go back to being what I have not been,
and learn to go back from such deeps
that amongst all natural things
I could live or not live; it does not matter
to be one stone more, the dark stone,
the pure stone which the river bears away.

[A.R.]

La memoria

Tengo que acordarme de todo,
recoger las briznas, los hilos
del acontecer harapiento
y metro a metro las moradas,
los largos caminos del tren,
la superficie del dolor.

Si se me extravía un rosal
y confundo noche con liebre
o bien se me desmoronó
todo un muro de la memoria
tengo que hacer de nuevo el aire,
el vapor, la tierra, las hojas,
el pelo y también los ladrillos,
las espinas que me clavaron,
la velocidad de la fuga.

Tengan piedad para el poeta.

Siempre olvidé con avidez
y en aquellas manos que tuve
sólo cabían inasibles
cosas que no se tocaban,
que se podían comparar
sólo cuando ya no existían.

Era el humo como un aroma,
era el aroma como el humo,
la piel de un cuerpo que dormía
y que despertó con mis besos,
pero no me pidan la fecha
ni el nombre de lo que soñé,
ni puedo medir el camino
que tal vez no tiene país
o aquella verdad que cambió
que tal vez se apagó de día
y fue luego luz errante
como en la noche una luciérnaga.

Memory

I have to remember everything,
keep track of blades of grass, the threads
of the untidy event, and
the houses, inch by inch,
the long lines of the railway,
the textured face of pain.

If I should get one rosebush wrong
and confuse night with a hare,
or even if one whole wall
has crumbled in my memory,
I have to make the air again,
steam, the earth, leaves,
hair and bricks as well,
the thorns which pierced me,
the speed of the escape.

Take pity on the poet.

I was always quick to forget
and in those hands of mine
grasped only the intangible
and unrelated things,
which could only be compared
by being non-existent.

The smoke was like an aroma,
the aroma was like smoke,
the skin of a sleeping body
which woke to my kisses;
but do not ask me the date
or the name of what I dreamed –
I cannot measure the road
which may have had no country,
or that truth which changed,
which the day perhaps subdued
to become a wandering light
like a firefly in the dark.

[A. R.]

from *Una casa en la arena* (1966)

La bandera

Mi bandera es azul y tiene un pez horizontal que encierran o desencierran dos círculos armilares. En invierno, con mucho viento y nadie por estos andurriales, me gusta oír la bandera restallando y el pescado nadando en el cielo como si viviera.

Y por qué ese pez, me preguntan. Es místico? Sí, les digo, es el simbólico ictiomín, el precristense, el cisternario, el lucicrático, el fritango, el verdadero, el frito, el pescado frito.

– Y nada más?

– Nada más.

Pero en el alto invierno allá arriba se debate la bandera con su pez en el aire temblando de frío, de viento, de cielo.

The Flag

My flag is blue and sports a fish rampant, locked in and let loose by two bracelets. In winter, when the wind blows hard and there's no one about in these out-of-the-way places, I like to hear the flag crack like a whip with the fish swimming in the sky as if it were alive.

And why this fish, I'm asked. Is it mystical? Yes, I say, it is the ichthyous symbol, the prechristic, the luminocratic, the friddled, the true, the fried, the fried fish.

– And nothing else?
– Nothing else.

But in high winter, the flag thrashes up there with its fish in the air, trembling with cold, wind and sky.

[N.T.]

from *La barcarola* (1967)

La barcarola termina

Sabréis que en aquella región que cruzaba con miedo
crispaba la noche los ruidos secretos, la sombra selvática,
y yo me arrastraba con los autobuses en el misterioso universo:
Asia negra, tiniebla del bosque, ceniza sagrada,
y mi juventud temblorosa con alas de mosca
saltando de aquí para allá por los reinos oscuros.

De pronto se inmovilizaron las ruedas, bajaron los desconocidos
y allí me quedé, occidental, en la soledad de la selva:
allí sin salir de aquel carro perdido en la noche,
con veinte años de edad esperando la muerte, refugiado en mi idioma.

De pronto un tambor en la selva, una antorcha, un rumor de la ruta,
y aquellos que predestiné como mis asesinos
bailaban allí, bajo el peso de la oscuridad de la selva,
para entretener al viajero perdido en remotas regiones.

Así cuando tantos presagios llevaban al fin de mi vida,
los altos tambores, las trenzas floridas, los centelleantes tobillos
danzaban sonriendo y cantando para un extranjero.

Te canto este cuento, amor mío, porque la enseñanza
del hombre se cumple a pesar del extraño atavío
y allí se fundaron en mí los principios del alba,
allí despertó mi razón a la fraternidad de los hombres.

Fue en Vietnam, en Vietnam en el año de mil novecientos veintiocho.

Cuarenta años después a la música de mis compañeros
llegó el gas asesino quemando los pies y la música,
quemando el silencio ritual de la naturaleza
incendiando el amor y matando la paz de los niños.

Maldición al atroz invasor! dice ahora el tambor reuniendo
al pequeño país en el nudo de su resistencia.

Amor mío, canté para ti los transcursos de mar y de día,
y fue soñolienta la luna de mi barcarola en el agua
porque lo dispuso el sistema de mi simetría

The Watersong Ends

You will know that in that region I once crossed fearfully
the night was stirring with secret sounds, darkness of jungle,
and I crawled along in a truck into that curious universe –
black Asia, forest dark, sacred ash,
and my youth trembling like the wings of a fly
darting from this place to that in uncertain kingdoms.

All at once the wheels came to a stop, the unknown ones climbed down
and there I was, a foreigner, in the solitudes of the jungle,
there, marooned in that truck stranded in night,
twenty years old, waiting for death, shrinking into my language.

Suddenly a drum began, a torch flared, there was a stirring,
and those I had taken for certain as my murderers
were dancing, beneath the towering dark of the jungle
to entertain a traveller strayed into those far regions.

So, when so many omens were pointing the end of my life,
the tall drum, the flowering tresses, the flashing ankles
were dancing and smiling and singing for a foreigner.

I tell you this story, love, because the lesson,
the human lesson, shines through its strange disguises
and there the principles of the dawn were grounded in me –
there my mind awoke to the sense of men as brothers.

That was in Vietnam, the Vietnam of 1928.

Forty years after, on the music of my companions
fell the murdering gas, scorching the feet and the music,
burning the ritual silence of the wilderness,
blasting love and destroying the peace of the children.

'Down with the brutish invader' sound the drums now, gathering
the tiny country into a knot of resistance.

My love, I told you all the happenings in the sea and the day,
and the moon in my watersong was dozing in the water.
The system of my symmetry had so arranged it

y el beso incitante de la primavera marina.
Te dije: a llevar por el mundo del viaje tus ojos amados!
La rosa que en mi corazón establece su pueblo fragante!
Y, dije, te doy además el recuerdo de pícaros y héroes,
el trueno del mundo acompaña con su poderío mis besos,
y así fue la barca barquera deslizándose en mi barcarola.

Pero años impuros, la sangre del hombre distante
recae en la espuma, nos mancha en la ola, salpica la luna: son nuestros,
son nuestros dolores aquellos distantes dolores
y la resistencia de los destruidos es parte concreta de mi alma.

Tal vez esta guerra se irá como aquellas que nos compartieron
dejándonos muertos, matándonos con los que mataron
pero el deshonor de este tiempo nos toca la frente con dedos quemados
y quién borrará lo inflexible que tuvo la sangre inocente?

Amor mío, a lo largo de la costa larga
de un pétalo a otro la tierra construye el aroma
y ya el estandarte de la primavera proclama
nuestra eternidad no por breve menos lacerante.

Si nunca la nave en su imperio regresa con dedos intactos,
si la barcarola seguía su rumbo en el trueno marino
y si tu cintura dorada vertió su belleza en mis manos
aquí sometemos en este regreso del mar, el destino,
y sin más examen cumplimos con la llamarada.

Quién oye la esencia secreta de la sucesión,
de la sucesiva estación que nos llena de sol o de llanto?
Escoge la tierra callada una hoja, la ramificada postrera
y cae en la altura amarilla como el testimonio de un advenimiento.

El hombre trepó a sus motores, se hicieron terribles
las obras de arte, los cuadros de plomo, las tristes estatuas de hilo,
los libros que se dedicaron a falsificar el relámpago,
los grandes negocios se hicieron con manchas de sangre en el barro de los
    arrozales,
y de la esperanza de muchos quedó un esqueleto imprevisto:
el fin de este siglo pagaba en el cielo lo que nos debía,
y mientras llegaba a la luna y dejaba caer herramientas de oro,

with the tingling first kiss of marine spring.
I told you – in carrying through my travelling world the vision of your eyes,
the rose in my heart sets up its own flowering place
and I said I give you as well memories of rogues and heroes,
all the thunder of the world rumbles beneath my kisses –
that was the way of the boat unwinding in my watersong.

But these are tainted years, ours; the blood of men far away
tumbles again in the foam, the waves stain us, the moon is spattered.
These faraway agonies are our agonies
and the struggle for the oppressed is a hard vein in my nature.

Perhaps this war will pass like the others which divided us,
leaving us dead, killing us along with the killers
but the shame of this time puts its burning fingers to our faces.
Who will erase the ruthlessness hidden in innocent blood?

My love, all along the broad coastline
from one petal to the next the earth yields up its aroma
and now the insignia of the spring is proclaiming
our eternity, no less painful for being brief.

If the ship never returns to port with its fingers uncalloused,
if the watersong followed its course in the thundering sea,
if your golden waist turned beautifully in my hands,
here let us submit to the seas' return, our destiny.
Without more ado, we comply with its tantrums.

Who can tune in to essential secrets of flow and succession
which in sequential stages fills us with sun, then weeping?
A leaf inclines to the great earth at its last branching
and falls in the yellow air as evidence of an advent.

Man turned to his mechanisms and made hideous
his works of art, his lead paintings, his wistful statues of wire,
his books which were aimed at falsifying the lightning;
business deals were made with stains of blood in the mud of the rice-fields,
and of the hopes of many only a faint skeleton remained –
in the sky, the end of the century was paying what it owed us.
And while they arrived on the moon and dropped tools of gold there,

no supimos nosotros, los hijos del lento crepúsculo,
si se descubría otra forma de muerte o teníamos un nuevo planeta.

Por mi parte y tu parte, cumplimos, compartimos esperanzas e inviernos
y fuimos heridos no sólo por los enemigos mortales
sino por mortales amigos (y esto pareció más amargo),
pero no me parece más dulce mi pan o mi libro entre tanto:
agregamos viviendo la cifra que falta al dolor
y seguimos amando el amor y con nuestra directa conducta
enterramos a los mentirosos y vivimos con los verdaderos.

Amor mío, la noche llegó galopando sobre las extensiones del mundo.

Amor mío, la noche borra el signo del mar y la nave resbala y reposa.

Amor mío, la noche encendió su instituto estrellado.

En el hueco del hombre dormido la mujer navegó desvelada
y bajaron los dos en el sueño por los ríos que llevan al llanto
y crecieron de nuevo entre los animales oscuros y los trenes cargados de sombra
hasta que no llegaron a ser sino pálidas piedras nocturnas.

Es la hora, amor mío, de apartar esta rosa sombría,
cerrar las estrellas, enterrar la ceniza en la tierra:
y en la insurrección de la luz, despertar con los que despertaron
o seguir en el sueño alcanzando la otra orilla del mar que no tiene otra orilla.

we never knew, children of the slow half-light,
if what was discovered was a new planet or a new form of death.

For my part and yours, we comply, we share our hopes and winters;
and we have been wounded not only by mortal enemies
but by mortal friends (that seemed all the more bitter),
but bread does not seem to taste sweeter, nor my book, in the meantime –
living, we supply the statistics that pain still lacks,
we go on loving love and in our blunt way
we bury the liars and live among the truth-tellers.

My love, night came down, galloping over the spread of the world.

My love, night erases all trace of the sea, the ship heels, is at rest.

My love, night lit up its starry institution.

To the place by the sleeping man, the woman glided in her wakefulness
and in dreams the two descended the rivers which led to the weeping
and grew once again among dark animals and trains loaded with shadows
to the point of being nothing more than pale stones at night.

It is time, love, to break off that sombre rose,
shut up the stars and bury the ash in the earth;
and, in the rising of the light, wake with those who awoke
or go on in the dream, reaching the other shore of the sea which has no other
    shore.

[A.R.]

MORE ABOUT PENGUINS
AND PELICANS

Penguinews, which appears every month, contains details of all the new books issued by Penguins as they are published. From time to time it is supplemented by the *Penguin Stock List*, which is our complete list of almost 5,000 titles.

A specimen copy of *Penguinews* will be sent to you free on request. Please write to Dept EP, Penguin Books Ltd, Harmondsworth, Middlesex, for your copy.

In the U.S.A.: For a complete list of books available from Penguins in the United States write to Dept CS, Penguin Books, 625 Madison Avenue, New York, New York 10022.

In Canada: For a complete list of books available from Penguins in Canada write to Penguin Books Canada Ltd, 2801 John Street, Markham, Ontario L3R 1B4.